Digital Image
Compression Techniques

Books in the SPIE Tutorial Texts Series

Digital Image Compression Techniques

Majid Rabbani
Paul W. Jones
Eastman Kodak Company

Donald C. O'Shea, Series Editor
Georgia Institute of Technology

TUTORIAL
TEXTS
IN OPTICAL
ENGINEERING

Volume TT 7

SPIE OPTICAL ENGINEERING PRESS

A Publication of SPIE—The International Society for Optical Engineering
Bellingham, Washington USA

Library of Congress Cataloging-in-Publication Data

Rabbani, Majid, 1955-
      Digital image compression techniques / Majid Rabbani and Paul W.
Jones.
           p. cm. — (Tutorial texts in optical engineering : v. TT 7)
      Includes bibliographical references.
      ISBN 0-8194-0648-1
      1. Image processing—Digital techniques. 2. Coding theory.
I. Jones, Paul W., 1958- . II. Title. III. Series.
TA1632.R23 1991
621.36´7—dc20   91-7509
                                                                                CIP

Published by
SPIE—The International Society for Optical Engineering
P.O. Box 10
Bellingham, Washington 98227-0010

Copyright © 1991 The Society of Photo-Optical Instrumentation Engineers

Printed in the United States of America

Second Printing

Introduction to the Series

These Tutorial Texts provide an introduction to specific optical technologies for both professionals and students. Based on selected SPIE short courses, they are intended to be accessible to readers with a basic physics or engineering background. Each text presents the fundamental theory to build a basic understanding as well as the information necessary to give the reader practical working knowledge. The included references form an essential part of each text for the reader requiring a more in-depth study.

Many of the books in the series will be aimed to readers looking for a concise tutorial introduction to new technical fields, such as CCDs, fiber optic amplifiers, sensor fusion, computer vision, or neural networks, where there may be only limited introductory material. Still others will present topics in classical optics tailored to the interests of a specific audience such as mechanical or electrical engineers. In this respect the Tutorial Text serves the function of a textbook. With its focus on a specialized or advanced topic, the Tutorial Text may also serve as a monograph, although with a marked emphasis on fundamentals.

As the series develops, a broad spectrum of technical fields will be represented. One advantage of this series and a major factor in the planning of future titles is our ability to cover new fields as they are developing, giving people the basic knowledge necessary to understand and apply new technologies.

Donald C. O'Shea   January 1991
Georgia Institute of Technology

To our precious wives, Mojgan and Teresa.

Contents

Preface

Information, in its many forms, is a valuable commodity in today's society, and the amount of information is increasing at a phenomenal rate. As a result, the ability to store, access, and transmit information in an efficient manner has become crucial. This is particularly true in the case of digital images. A large number of bits is typically required to represent even a single digital image, and with the rapid advances in sensor technology and digital electronics, this number grows larger with each new generation of products. Furthermore, the number of digital images created each day increases as more applications are found.

In order to utilize digital images effectively, specific techniques are needed to reduce the number of bits required for their representation. The branch of digital image processing that deals with this problem is called image compression (also picture coding). A wide range of techniques has been developed over the years, and novel approaches continue to emerge. The goal of this book is to lay the groundwork for understanding image compression techniques and to present a number of specific schemes that have proven to be useful. The algorithms discussed in this book are mainly concerned with the compression of continuous-tone, still-frame, monochrome and color images. A consistent image set has been used to illustrate the effect of each compression technique on typical images, thus allowing for a direct comparison of bit rates and reconstructed image quality. However, an important point to consider when viewing these images is that due to limitations of the printing reproduction process, the resolution of these printed images may not be adequate to reveal subtle differences between the various techniques.

This book is divided into four parts. Part I is an introduction to the process of digital image formation and outlines the need for image compression as well as related worldwide standardization activities. Part II presents an overview of information theory concepts commonly used in image compression. The approach in this part is to give the reader a feel for the utility of information theory, and no attempt is made to be mathematically rigorous. The concepts are of general utility in the compression of both bilevel and continuous-tone images. Part III describes techniques for the lossless compression of images, that is, techniques that allow the original image to be reconstructed exactly after compression. Part IV covers the field of lossy image compression as applied to still, continuous-tone images, where much lower bit rates are achieved as compared to lossless techniques, at the expense of errors in the reconstructed image. This part also includes a chapter on hierarchical coding techniques (which may be lossless or lossy). Finally, an appendix on the compression of color images is included.

Acknowledgments

The authors would like to acknowledge our colleagues, Paul Melnychuck and Scott Daly of the Image Coding and Restoration Group at Eastman Kodak Company, who provided valuable insights and information during the writing of this book. We also thank the management of Eastman Kodak Company, and in particular Terry Lund, for providing the necessary resources and support. The comments provided by our reviewers and editors are also gratefully acknowledged.

Part I

Background

Chapter 1

Digital Images and Image Compression

The demand for handling images in digital form has increased dramatically in recent years. Thanks to performance improvements and significant reductions in the cost of image scanners, photographs, printed text, and other media can now be easily converted into digital form (*image digitization*). Direct acquisition of digital images (*scene digitization*) is also becoming more common as sensors and associated electronics improve; the use of satellite imaging, e.g., LANDSAT, in remote sensing of the earth and the advent of electronic still-cameras in the consumer market are good examples. In addition, many different imaging modalities in medicine, such as computed tomography (CT) or magnetic resonance imaging (MRI), generate images directly in digital form. Computer-generated images (*synthetic images*) are also becoming a major source of digital data. The use of computer graphics in advertising and entertainment is widespread, and its use in scientific visualization and engineering applications is growing at a rapid pace. The reason for this interest in digital images is clear: representing images in digital form allows visual information to be easily manipulated in useful and novel ways. This fact, combined with the exponential growth in computing power over the past decade, has resulted in the use of digital imaging systems in such diverse fields as astronomy, remote sensing, medicine, photojournalism, graphic arts, law enforcement, advertisement, and manufacturing.

Despite the advantages, there is one potential problem with digital images, namely, the large number of bits required to represent them. Fortunately, digital images, in their canonical representation, generally contain a significant amount of redundancy. Image compression, which is the art/science of efficient coding of picture data, aims at taking advantage of this redundancy to reduce the number of bits required to represent an image. This can result in significant savings in the memory needed for image storage or in the channel capacity required for image transmission. Several excellent review articles on image compression have been published in the literature [1-4]. There have also been several special journal issues dedicated to image coding and visual communications [5-12]. A few books are wholly devoted to the subject [13-16], and numerous textbooks on image processing also contain detailed coverage of image compression [17-21].

1.1   Digital Image Formation

The source for a digital image may be a 3-D scene in the real world, or it may be a 2-D image generated previously, e.g., a photograph. In either case, the information in the source is analog in that it is continuous in both space and amplitude. To generate a digital image, the source is first sampled at discrete locations using some type of sensor (or sensors, if color or multispectral data are required)[22]. These samples are termed *pixels* or *pels* (for *picture elements*). The pixel values produced by the sensor are continuous over some finite range, and they are usually linearly related to the radiant energy intensity at each sampled location. The use of the term radiant energy (rather than light) is deliberate since the sensor may be sensitive to wavelengths outside of the range of human vision. In the case of an image that has been generated previously (such as a photograph or transparency), the radiant energy is the result of an illumination source impinging on the image and being reflected or transmitted to the sensor.

Different strategies are possible for the sampling locations, but the most common is an equispaced rectangular grid. Ideally, each sample corresponds to an infinitesimally small region of the source, but because of the physical nature of sensors and associated optics, it is actually an integrated value over some finite area. The number of sampled locations per unit area defines the *sampling rate* of the system, and this sampling rate should be chosen based on the Nyquist sampling theorem; i.e., the sampling rate should be at least twice the highest spatial frequency component of the source. If this criterion is not met, the sampled image will contain *aliasing* artifacts generated when spatial frequencies higher than $1/2$ the sampling rate appear as lower frequencies. To prevent aliasing, a prefilter can be used in the system to limit the bandwidth of the source prior to sampling. (Note that the integration performed by the sensor also acts as a prefilter.) In image digitization systems, the sampling rate is often given in terms of the *scanning resolution*, which is the inverse of the sampling rate. In general, the required scanning resolution depends on the application. For example, for a 14×17-inch radiograph viewed by a radiologist at a typical distance of 14 inches, a scanning resolution of 70 μm/pixel that captures spatial frequencies as high as 7 cycles/mm is adequate (based on data for the human visual system (HVS) contrast sensitivity function [23]). For a 35-mm negative, subject to subsequent magnification and processing, a scanning resolution of 12 μm/pixel is more typical.

Each continuous-valued sampled point is quantized to one of a discrete number of levels in order to form the digital image. It is well known that uniform changes in intensity values are not perceived equally by the HVS. For example, uniform quantization of the intensity values (i.e., quantization in linear space) can result in visually apparent quantization errors in the dark areas [24]. Since images are viewed by human subjects in most applications, it is important to perform the quantization in a domain that is in accordance with the HVS perception. In many cases, the pixel values are subjected to a nonlinearity (such as a logarithm or a cube-root function) prior to quantization that approximates the nonlinearity in the HVS. The number of quantization levels required to adequately represent an image is also dependent on the application. For binary text documents, only two levels (1 bit/pixel) are required since each sampled point would either be black or white. For natural scenes or continuous-tone photographs, it is common to use 8 bits/pixel (256 levels). However, depending on the dynamic range of the source and the type of sensor output (e.g., linear or log), it may be necessary to use 10 or 12 bits/pixel. In fact, to overcome the inaccuracy associated with the direct analog implementation of the nonlinearity, more sophisticated image digitizers first use 12-14 bits to quantize the pixel values in the linear space, apply the nonlinearity to the digital data, and then requantize to 8 bits using a look-up table.

1.2   The Need for Image Compression

The need for image compression becomes apparent when one computes the number of bits per image resulting from typical sampling rates and quantization schemes. For example, consider the amount of storage required for the following types of images:

- a low-resolution, TV quality, color video image: 512×512 pixels/color, 8 bits/pixel, and 3 colors $\implies \approx 6 \times 10^6$ bits,

- a 24×36-mm (35-mm) negative photograph scanned at 12 μm: 3000×2000 pixels/color, 8 bits/pixel, and 3 colors $\implies \approx 144 \times 10^6$ bits,

- a 14×17-inch radiograph scanned at 70 μm: 5000×6000 pixels, 12 bits/pixel, $\implies \approx 360 \times 10^6$ bits,

- a LANDSAT Thematic Mapper scene (used in remote sensing): approximately 6000×6000 pixels/spectral band, 8 bits/pixel, and 6 nonthermal spectral bands $\implies \approx 1.7 \times 10^9$ bits.

Obviously, the storage of even a few images could pose a problem. As another example of the need for image compression, consider the transmission of the low-resolution $512 \times 512 \times 8$ bits/pixel $\times$ 3-color video image over telephone lines. Using a 9600 baud (bits/s) modem, the transmission would take approximately 11 minutes for just a single image, which is unacceptable for most applications.

1.3   Classification of Compression Techniques

The examples in the preceding section clearly illustrate how the digitization process results in a large number of bits for each image. However, the number of bits actually required to represent the information in an image may be substantially less because of redundancy. In general, three types of redundancy in digital images can be identified:

- spatial redundancy, which is due to the correlation (or dependence) between neighboring pixel values,

- spectral redundancy, which is due to the correlation between different color planes (e.g., in an RGB color image) or spectral bands (e.g., aerial photographs in remote sensing),

- temporal redundancy, which is due to the correlation between different frames in a sequence of images.

Image compression research aims to reduce the number of bits required to represent an image by removing these redundancies. In addition, it seeks to establish fundamental limits on the performance of any compression scheme for a given class of images. This is done using *information theory* concepts, which are discussed in Part II of this book. Beyond these basic goals, it is also necessary to develop a variety of algorithms suited to different applications. There are many approaches to image compression, but they can be categorized into two fundamental groups: *lossless* and *lossy*.

In lossless compression (also known as *bit-preserving* or *reversible* compression), the reconstructed image after compression is numerically identical to the original image on a pixel-by-pixel basis. Obviously, lossless compression is ideally desired since no information is compromised. However, only a modest amount of compression is possible. Lossless compression techniques are the subject of Part III of this book.

In lossy compression (also known as *irreversible* compression), the reconstructed image contains degradations relative to the original. As a result, much higher compression can be achieved as compared to lossless compression. In general, more compression is obtained at the expense of more distortion. It is important to note that these degradations may or may not be visually apparent. In fact, the term *visually lossless* has often been used to characterize lossy compression schemes that result in no visible loss under normal viewing conditions. Unfortunately, the definition of visually lossless is quite subjective and extreme caution should be taken in its interpretation. It is conceivable that an algorithm that is visually lossless under certain viewing conditions, e.g., a 19-inch video monitor viewed at a distance of 4 feet, could result in visible degradations under more stringent viewing conditions such as a 14 × 17-inch secondary image printed on film. Lossy compression techniques are the subject of Part IV of this book.

These two categories can be further divided based on the nature of the original input image. The image may be either binary, e.g., text and documents, or continuous-tone, e.g., 8-bit video, 12-bit medical images, etc. It may be either a still image, which contains spatial redundancy (and spectral redundancy if a color image), or it may be a sequence of images, e.g., motion pictures, which contains temporal redundancy as well. The focus of this book is on lossless and lossy techniques for still-frame, continuous-tone, monochrome and color images. The issue of image sequence compression is not addressed specifically, but many of the techniques that are described for still images are applicable to sequence compression.

1.4   Effect of Digitization Parameters on Compression

The redundancy present in a digital image is highly dependent on the system used to form the image as well as on the parameters used to represent it. In particular, the sampling rate, the number of quantization levels, and the presence of source and/or sensor noise can all affect the achievable compression. Although variations will exist from image to image, the following trends are generally found for statistically based compression algorithms:

- As the sampling rate is increased, pixel-to-pixel correlations increase, which allow for a higher compression ratio.[1] The compression ratio (CR) is defined to be

$$CR = \frac{\text{Number of bits for original image}}{\text{Number of bits for compressed image}}. \qquad (1.1)$$

  This increase in pixel-to-pixel correlation means, for example, that if the sampling rate is increased by factor of two, the increase in the number of bits required for the compressed image will be less than a factor of two (although the total number of bits will still increase).

- Increasing the number of quantization levels reduces the pixel-to-pixel correlations to some extent, thus reducing the achievable compression.

---

[1]For image digitization systems, a higher sampling rate amounts to a smaller scanning aperture. Since the variance of the noise due to granularity of the film is inversely proportional to the aperture size, a higher sampling rate results in a larger noise variance. The negative effect that the higher noise has on the compressibility is ignored here.

- The presence of any source noise (for example, film grain noise in a photographic print) or noise introduced by the sensor will decrease the pixel-to-pixel correlations and reduce the amount of achievable compression.

In later chapters, we discuss a number of different compression techniques and present results for actual images. In light of the previous comments, it is important to keep in mind that the results presented in this book (and for that matter, the results presented in any other book or paper on image compression) are specific to the particular image being compressed. The particular images that will be used in this book to illustrate the various techniques are shown in Fig. 1.1. Both are 512×512 monochrome images with 8 bits/pixel and are referred to as LENA (top image) and BOOTS (bottom image).

1.5   Image Compression Standardization Activities

The only widely used digital image compression standards in existence today are the international digital facsimile Group 3 and Group 4 coding standards established by the working group of the Consultative Committee of the International Telephone and Telegraph (CCITT) [25]. These standards are only applicable to bilevel images such as text and documents and cannot be used for the compression of continuous-tone images or image sequences. However, the ever-increasing need to handle such images in digital form across many diverse applications has made additional compression standards inevitable. The adoption of such standards not only facilitates the exchange of images across application boundaries, but also helps to reduce significantly the cost of the specialized hardware required in many real time image compression systems. Currently, image compression standardization efforts are focused in three areas:

- **Bilevel images:**

  A committee known as JBIG (for Joint Bilevel Imaging Group) was formed under the joint auspices of ISO-IEC/JTC1/SC2/WG8 [2] and CCITT SGVIII NIC [3] in 1988 to work on a standard for the compression and decompression of bilevel images. Since the CCITT Group 3 and Group 4 standards already existed in this area, the group's primary focus was to seek an algorithm that would outperform the existing standard within its scope of applicability (e.g., on the eight CCITT

---

[2]International Standardization Organization, Joint Technical Committee 1, Character Sets and Coding Subcommittee, Working Group 8 (Coded Representation of Picture and Audio Information).

[3]Study Group VIII Special Rapporteur Group on New Forms of Image Communication.

Figure 1.1: Original LENA (top) and BOOTS (bottom).

bilevel reference images), and also extend its utility to other applications. For example, a mandatory requirement of the standard is the capability for the progressive representation of images, an indispensable feature in an environment where the compressed data are made available to a number of display or transmission devices with varying degrees of resolution and/or quality requirements. In addition, the standard algorithm should be adaptive so that it can efficiently compress images with different characteristics. For example, when the existing facsimile standards are used to compress digitally halftoned images, as much as a 50% data expansion can occur since the current standard uses predefined coding tables based on the statistics of binary documents and text. The JBIG-proposed algorithm successfully compresses this type of data.

- **Continuous-tone, still-frame, monochrome and color images:**

  A committee known as JPEG (for Joint Photographic Experts Group) was formed under the joint auspices of ISO-IEC/JTC1/SC2/WG8 and CCITT SGVIII NIC at the end of 1986 for the purpose of developing an international standard for the compression and decompression of continuous-tone, still-frame, monochrome and color images. A major motivation for the formation of JPEG was the advent of multimedia services on the 64 Kbits/s Integrated Services Digital Networks (ISDN). The goal of this committee is to define a standard for applications as diverse as photo-videotex, desktop publishing, graphic arts, color facsimile, photojournalism, medical systems, and many others. Although no standards existed previously in these areas, JPEG members had the strong conviction that the requirements of most of these applications could be satisfied by a common, general-purpose image compression standard. The proposed JPEG standard consists of three main components: 1) a baseline system that provides a simple and efficient algorithm that is adequate for most image coding applications, 2) a set of extended system features such as progressive build-up that allows the baseline system to satisfy a broader range of applications, and 3) an independent lossless method for applications requiring that type of compression. A detailed description of the proposed JPEG baseline system is included in Chapter 10 of this book.

- **Sequential, continuous-tone images:**

  Recently, CCITT has standardized a coding algorithm for video telephony and video conferencing at bit rates ranging from 64 to 1920 Kbits/s [26]. Since 1988, a standardization group known as MPEG (for Moving Picture Experts Group) has also been working under the auspices of ISO-IEC/JTC1/SC2/WG8 to develop a standard for storage and retrieval of moving images and sound using digital storage media with a combined bit rate of 1.0-1.5 Mbits/s. The MPEG standard aims to be a general-purpose technique for applications as diverse as electronic publishing, travel guidance, (video)^2 text, education, games, entertainment, video mail, and teleseminar training.

References

[1] M. Kunt, A. Ikonomopoulos, and M. Kocher, "Second-generation image-coding techniques," Proc. IEEE, 73(4), 549-574 (1985).

[2] A. K. Jain, "Image data compression: a review," Proc. IEEE, 69(3), 349-389 (1981).

[3] A. N. Netravali, "Picture coding: a review," Proc. IEEE, 68(3), 366-406 (1980).

[4] A. Habibi, "Survey of adaptive image coding techniques," IEEE Trans. Commun., COM-25(11), 1275-1284 (1977).

[5] T. R. Hsing and K.-H. Tzou, eds., Special Issue on Visual Communications and Image Processing, Opt. Eng., 28(7) (1989).

[6] T. R. Hsing, ed., Special Issue on Visual Communications and Image Processing, Opt. Eng., 26(7), (1987).

[7] A. N. Netravali and B. Prasada, eds., Special Issue on Visual Communication Systems, Proc. IEEE, 73(4), 497-848 (1985).

[8] A. N. Netravali and A. Habibi, eds., Special Issue on Picture Communication Systems, IEEE Trans. Commun., COM-29(12), 1725-2008 (1981).

[9] A. N. Netravali, ed., Special Issue on Digital Encoding of Graphics, Proc. IEEE, 68(7), (1980).

[10] A. Habibi, ed., Special Issue on Image Bandwidth Compression, IEEE Trans. Commun., COM-25(11), (1977).

[11] H. C. Andrews and L. H. Enloe, eds., Special Issue on Digital Picture Processing, Proc. IEEE, 60(7), 763-922 (1972).

[12] M. R. Aaron, ed., Special Issue on Signal Processing for Digital Communications, Part I, IEEE Trans. Commun. Tech., COM-19(6), 870-1156 (1971).

[13] A. N. Netravali and B. G. Haskell, *Digital Pictures: Representation and Compression,* Plenum Press, New York (1988).

[14] R. J. Clarke, *Transform Coding of Images,* Academic Press, London (1985).

[15] N. S. Jayant and P. Noll, *Digital Coding of Waveforms,* Prentice-Hall, Englewood Cliffs, NJ (1984).

[16] W. K. Pratt, ed., *Image Transmission Techniques, Advances in Electronics and Electron Physics,* Supplement 12, Academic Press, Orlando, FL (1979).

[17] J. S. Lim, *Two-dimensional Signal and Image Processing,* Prentice-Hall, Englewood Cliffs, NJ (1990).

[18] A. K. Jain, *Fundamentals of Digital Image Processing,* Prentice-Hall, Englewood Cliffs, NJ (1989).

[19] R. C. Gonzalez and P. Wintz, *Digital Image Processing,* 2nd Edition, Addison-Wesley, Reading, MA (1987).

[20] A. Rosenfeld and A. C. Kak, *Digital Picture Processing,* Vol. 1, Academic Press, Orlando, FL (1982).

[21] W. K. Pratt, *Digital Image Processing,* Wiley-Interscience, New York (1978).

[22] J. R. Milch, "Image Scanning and Digitization," in *Imaging Processes and Materials,* J. Sturge, V. Walworth, and A. Shepp, eds., Neblette's 8th Edition, 292-321, Van Nostrand Reinhold, New York (1989).

[23] P. G. J. Barten, "The SQRI method: a new method for the evaluation of visible resolution on a display," Proc. SID, 28(3), 253-262 (1987).

[24] M. I. Sezan, K.-L. Yip, and S. J. Daly, "Uniform perceptual quantization: applications to digital radiography," IEEE Trans. Syst. Man Cyber., SMC-17(4), 622-634 (1987).

[25] R. Hunter and A. H. Robinson, "International digital facsimile coding standards," Proc. of the IEEE, 68(7), 854-867 (1980).

[26] "Draft Revision of Recommendation H.261," Document 572, CCITT SG XV, Working Party XV/1, Special Group on Coding for Visual Telephony.

Part II

Information Theory Concepts

Chapter 2

Source Models and Entropy

Any information-generating process can be viewed as a source that emits a sequence of symbols chosen from a finite alphabet. For example, this text has been generated by a source with an alphabet that contains all the ASCII symbols. Similarly, a computer performs its computations on binary data, and such data may be considered as a sequence of symbols generated by a source with a binary alphabet composed of 0 and 1.

In the case of images, one may think of an n-bit image as being generated by a source with an alphabet of 2^n symbols representing the possible code values. The ordering of the sequence produced by an image source might correspond to adjacent pixel values based on a 1-D raster scan, or it might correspond to values taken from a 2-D block of pixels. It is advantageous to develop models for image sources in order to measure the "information" conveyed by these sequences of symbols. In the following chapters, we examine several source models and related information theory concepts that are useful in image compression.

2.1 Discrete Memoryless Sources

The simplest form of an information source is the *discrete memoryless source* (DMS), in which successive symbols produced by the source are statistically independent. A DMS S is completely specified by its source alphabet $S = \{s_1, s_2, \cdots, s_n\}$ and the associated probabilities of occurrence $\{p(s_1), p(s_2), \cdots, p(s_n)\}$. An important quantity is the *average information* provided by a DMS. Before defining this quantity, we should first address the question of what is meant by the "information" contained in a certain event. Of course, any definition of information is only useful if it can serve as a tool to solve problems, and our measure of information, whatever it may

15

be, should have some intuitive properties. For instance, it is reasonable to assume that the occurrence of a less probable event (symbol) should provide more information than the occurrence of a more probable event. Furthermore, the information of independent (unrelated) events taken as a single event should equal the sum of the information of such events. If we agree to define $I(s_i)$, the information revealed by the occurrence of a certain source symbol s_i, in terms of its probability $p(s_i)$, then there is only one definition that is consistent with the above intuitive properties, namely,

$$I(s_i) = \log \frac{1}{p(s_i)}. \tag{2.1}$$

The base of the logarithm determines the units used to express the amount of information. If base two is used, the information is in binary units or bits. If we average this quantity over all possible source symbols of the DMS, we find the average amount of information per source symbol, $H(S)$, also known as the *entropy*, i.e.,

$$H(S) = \sum_{i=1}^{n} p(s_i) I(s_i) = - \sum_{i=1}^{n} p(s_i) \log_2 p(s_i) \qquad \text{bits/symbol.} \tag{2.2}$$

As an example, consider a DMS S with four source symbols: $S = \{A, B, C, D\}$ with $P(A) = 0.60$, $P(B) = 0.30$, $P(C) = 0.05$, and $P(D) = 0.05$. Using Eq. (2.2), we find $H(S) = 1.40$ bits/symbol.

The entropy of a source may be interpreted in two ways. By definition, it is the average amount of information per source symbol provided by the source. It can also be interpreted as the average amount of information per source symbol that an observer needs to spend to remove the uncertainty in the source. For instance, an observer may attempt to determine an unknown source symbol by asking questions requiring simple yes-or-no answers. Each question is then equivalent to spending one bit of information. The observer may design sophisticated schemes aimed at minimizing the average number of questions necessary to reveal each symbol or even ask questions designed to reveal several source symbols at one time. However, no matter how sophisticated the scheme used, it can never reveal source symbols with an *average* number of binary questions (or bits) per symbol less than the entropy of the source.

2.2   Extensions of a Discrete Memoryless Source

It is often useful to deal with blocks of symbols rather than individual symbols. Consider a DMS S with an alphabet of size n where the output of the source is grouped into blocks of N symbols. Each block may be considered as a single source symbol generated by a source S^N with an alphabet of size n^N. The source S^N is called the Nth *extension of the source* S.

Since we are dealing with a memoryless source, the probability of a symbol $\sigma_i = (s_{i_1}, s_{i_2}, \cdots, s_{i_N})$ from S^N is given by $p(\sigma_i) = p(s_{i_1})p(s_{i_2}) \cdots p(s_{i_N})$. It can be shown that the entropy per extended source symbol of S^N is N times the entropy per individual symbol of S, i.e.,

$$H(S^N) = NH(S). \tag{2.3}$$

2.3 Markov Sources

The DMS considered in the previous section is too restrictive for many applications. In general, the previous part of a message can significantly influence the probabilities for the next symbol; that is, the source has memory. For instance, in English text the letter Q is almost always followed by the letter U; thus the probability of seeing the letter U is greatly influenced by the letter that precedes it. In digital images, the analogous situation is where the probability of a given pixel taking on a particular code value is dependent on the surrounding pixel values. Such a source can be modeled as a *Markov source*. An mth-order Markov source is a source in which the probability of occurrence of a source symbol s_i depends upon a finite number m of the preceding symbols. It is specified by the set of conditional probabilities

$$p(s_i|s_{j_1}, s_{j_2}, \cdots, s_{j_m}) \qquad \text{where} \qquad i, j_p(p = 1, \cdots, m) = 1, 2, \cdots, n.$$

It is useful to consider a Markov source as being in some state which depends on the preceding m symbols. For a first-order Markov source, there are n states, one for each symbol s_i of the source alphabet. For a second-order Markov source, there are n^2 states, one for every pair of symbols from the source alphabet. In general, an mth-order Markov source has n^m states. For an ergodic Markov source (the kind with practical interest to us), there is a unique probability distribution over the set of states which is known as the *stationary* or *equilibrium distribution*. One way of illustrating a Markov source is by the use of a state diagram, where each state is represented by a circle, and the possible transitions from state to state are represented by arrows connecting the circles. The transition probabilities are indicated by the numbers alongside the arrows. An example of a state diagram is shown in Fig. 2.1 for a second-order Markov source with a binary alphabet.

To compute the entropy of the mth-order Markov source, we first find $H(S|s_{j_1}, s_{j_2}, \cdots, s_{j_m})$, the source entropy given that it is in a particular state $(s_{j_1}, s_{j_2}, \cdots, s_{j_m})$, using

$$H(S|s_{j_1}, s_{j_2}, \cdots, s_{j_m}) = -\sum_{i=1}^{n} p(s_i|s_{j_1}, \cdots, s_{j_m}) \log p(s_i|s_{j_1}, \cdots, s_{j_m}). \tag{2.4}$$

These conditional entropies are then weighted by the corresponding probability of being in that state and summed over all possible states, i.e.,

$$H(S) = \sum_{S^m} p(s_{j_1}, s_{j_2}, \cdots, s_{j_m}) H(S|s_{j_1}, s_{j_2}, \cdots, s_{j_m}). \qquad (2.5)$$

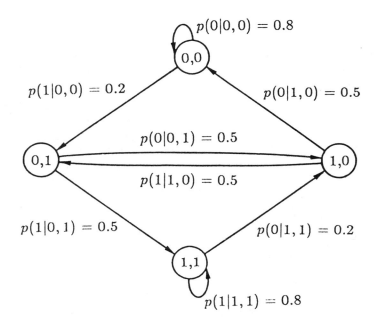

Figure 2.1: Markov process state diagram.

2.3.1   Example

Consider the second-order Markov source with a binary source alphabet $S = \{0, 1\}$ shown in Fig. 2.1. The conditional symbol probabilities are

$$p(0|0,0) = p(1|1,1) = 0.8, \qquad (2.6)$$

$$p(1|0,0) = p(0|1,1) = 0.2, \qquad (2.7)$$

$$p(0|0,1) = p(0|1,0) = p(1|1,0) = p(1|0,1) = 0.5. \qquad (2.8)$$

There are four possible states which are represented by (0,0), (0,1), (1,0), and (1,1). Because of symmetry, the stationary probability distribution of these states satisfies

$$p(0,0) = p(1,1) \qquad (2.9)$$

and

$$p(0,1) = p(1,0). \qquad (2.10)$$

Also, the source has to be in some state at any given time, so

$$p(0,0) + p(0,1) + p(1,0) + p(1,1) = 1. \tag{2.11}$$

Now, there are two transitions that can take the source into the state (0,0). One is if the source emits a 0 while it is in state (0,0) (which occurs with probability 0.8), and the other is if the source emits a 0 while it is in state (1,0) (which occurs with the probability 0.5). A similar argument concerning the state (0,1) leads to the following equations:

$$p(0,0) = 0.5p(0,1) + 0.8p(0,0), \tag{2.12}$$

$$p(0,1) = 0.2p(0,0) + 0.5p(0,1). \tag{2.13}$$

Simultaneous solution of these equations results in

$$p(0,0) = p(1,1) = \frac{5}{14}, \qquad p(0,1) = p(1,0) = \frac{2}{14}, \tag{2.14}$$

which are the stationary probabilities of the Markov source. We can now construct Table 2.1 and compute the entropy of this source:

$$H(S) = -\sum_{2^3} p(s_{i_1}, s_{i_2}, s_i) \log_2 p(s_i | s_{i_1}, s_{i_2}) = 0.801 \quad \text{bit/symbol}. \tag{2.15}$$

s_{i_1}	s_{i_2}	s_{i_3}	$p(s_i \| s_{i_1}, s_{i_2})$	$p(s_{i_1}, s_{i_2})$	$p(s_{i_1}, s_{i_2}, s_i)$
0	0	0	0.8	5/14	4/14
0	0	1	0.2	5/14	1/14
0	1	0	0.5	2/14	1/14
0	1	1	0.5	2/14	1/14
1	0	0	0.5	2/14	1/14
1	0	1	0.5	2/14	1/14
1	1	0	0.2	5/14	1/14
1	1	1	0.8	5/14	4/14

Table 2.1: Markov source probabilities.

2.4 Extensions of a Markov Source and Adjoint Sources

The *Nth extension of a Markov source*, S^N, is a μth-order Markov source with symbols defined as blocks of N symbols from the original source, where $\mu = \lceil m/N \rceil$.[1] As in the case of a DMS, the entropy of an extended

---

[1] $\lceil x \rceil$ is the smallest integer larger than x.

Markov source, S^N, is N times the entropy of the original source, S, i.e., $H(S^N) = NH(S)$. Another useful concept is that of the *adjoint source*. Consider first the Nth extension of a Markov source, S^N, with source symbols $\{\sigma_1, \sigma_2, \cdots, \sigma_{n^N}\}$ and stationary probabilities $\{p(\sigma_1), p(\sigma_2), \cdots, p(\sigma_{n^N})\}$, and now consider a DMS with the same alphabet and the same symbol probabilities. This DMS is called the adjoint source of S^N and is denoted by $\overline{S^N}$. In effect, the adjoint source ignores the conditional probabilities which describe the dependence between the extended symbols. An interesting property of the adjoint source is that its entropy, $H(\overline{S^N})$, is always larger than the entropy of its corresponding extended Markov source, $H(S^N)$, i.e.,

$$H(\overline{S^N}) \geq H(S^N). \tag{2.16}$$

This is intuitive since the adjoint source, being a DMS, is not constrained by the restrictions imposed on a Markov source. This lack of structure makes the output of the DMS source less predictable (more uncertain), and hence increases its entropy. It can be shown that the entropy per original source symbol of the adjoint source, $H_N(S)$, approaches the entropy of the Markov source as the block size N goes to infinity, i.e.,

$$\lim_{N \to \infty} H_N(S) = \lim_{N \to \infty} \frac{H(\overline{S^N})}{N} = H(S). \tag{2.17}$$

Note that the adjoint source of any DMS is the DMS itself.

2.4.1   Example

Consider the Markov source S with the state diagram given in Fig. 2.1. The adjoint source, $\overline{S}$, is a DMS with alphabet $\{0, 1\}$. Because of symmetry, $p(0) = p(1) = 0.5$, so $H_1(S) = H(\overline{S}) = 1$ bit/symbol. This implies that an observer who models this source as a DMS and is ignorant of the Markov structure, measures an entropy of 1 bit/symbol for the source. The adjoint source $\overline{S^2}$, which corresponds to the 2nd extension of S, is a DMS with four symbols. The symbol probabilities are given in Eq. (2.14). The entropy per original source symbol, $H_2(S)$, of this source is 0.932 bits. Finally, $\overline{S^3}$ is a DMS with an alphabet of eight symbols with probabilities given by the last column of Table 2.1. Its entropy per original source symbol, $H_3(S)$, is found to be 0.888 bits. We see that as N increases, the entropy per original source symbol of the adjoint source, $H_N(S)$, approaches 0.801, the entropy of the second-order Markov source.

2.5   The Noiseless Source Coding Theorem

We now consider a variation of the *noiseless source coding theorem* that concerns the encoding of blocks of source symbols into binary codewords. Let S be an ergodic source with an alphabet of size n and an entropy $H(S)$. Consider encoding blocks of N source symbols at a time into binary codewords. For any $\delta > 0$, it is possible, by choosing N large enough, to construct a code in such a way that the average number of bits per original source symbol, $\overline{L}$, satisfies

$$H(S) \leq \overline{L} < H(S) + \delta. \tag{2.18}$$

Furthermore, the left-hand inequality must be satisfied for any uniquely decodable code for the block of N source symbols.

This theorem states that any source can be losslessly encoded with a code whose average number of bits per source symbol is arbitrarily close to, but not less than, the source entropy in bits. However, to get arbitrarily close to the entropy, one usually has to encode higher extensions of the source. In the next chapter, we discuss methods of constructing codes that achieve performance close to the entropy.

Chapter 3

Variable-Length Codes

While the noiseless coding theorem provides for the existence of a code that can achieve a rate equal to or approaching the entropy of a source, it unfortunately does not provide a means for constructing an actual code. Generally, *variable-length codes* are used together with source extensions to achieve the desired performance. In this chapter, we discuss the use and construction of variable-length codes for source encoding.

Consider an example in which a DMS S has four symbols, s_1, s_2, s_3, and s_4, with probabilities given in Table 3.1. We wish to construct an efficient code using a binary alphabet to encode this source. Our code should have some desired characteristics. For instance, each codeword in the sequence should be instantaneously decodable, i.e., decodable without reference to the succeeding codewords. A necessary and sufficient condition for constructing such codes is that no codeword be a prefix of some other codeword. Any code satisfying this condition is called a *prefix condition code*. Code I in Table 3.1, which is a fixed-length code, has an average length of 2 bits/symbol and is clearly a prefix condition code. Since the entropy of the source, $H(S)$, is only 1.40 bits/symbol, according to the noiseless source coding theorem,

Symbol	Probability	Code I	Code II
s_1	0.60	00	0
s_2	0.30	01	10
s_3	0.05	10	110
s_4	0.05	11	111

Table 3.1: Fixed-length and variable-length codes for S.

one should be able to construct more efficient codes with an average length arbitrarily close to that value. Consider constructing a variable-length code for the source S with $l(s_i)$ denoting the length of the codeword assigned to the symbol s_i. To minimize the average length of the code, $\overline{L}$, it is desirable to assign the shortest codewords to the most probable symbols. Since the entropy of the source is $\sum_i p(s_i)I(s_i)$ and the average length of the code is

$$\overline{L} = \sum_{i=1}^{n} p(s_i)l(s_i), \tag{3.1}$$

the codeword lengths should be chosen so that

$$l(s_i) = I(s_i) = -\log_2 p(s_i) \quad \text{bits.} \tag{3.2}$$

In this way, the code results in a rate equal to the entropy. Unfortunately, this is only possible if $-\log_2 p(s_i)$ is an integer. It seems reasonable that a good code would arise if the $l(s_i)$ values are chosen to be the smallest integer greater than this value[1]; i.e., set $l(s_i) = -\lceil \log_2 p(s_i) \rceil$. This approach is known as *Shannon-Fano coding*. Although it does not generally result in the best code, it can serve as a guideline for choosing the codeword lengths. In our example, it results in codeword lengths of 1, 2, 5, and 5 for s_1, s_2, s_3, and s_4, respectively. Using this as a guide, we start by assigning '0' to the symbol s_1. Since no other codeword may start with '0', we assign the next shortest codeword, '10', to s_2. We do not need to spend 5 bits for s_3 and s_4 since we can encode them with only 3 bits. Code II in Table 3.1 illustrates this code. The average length of the code is 1.5 bits/symbol. We may try constructing other variable-length codes for this source (an infinite number of such codes exist), but none would have an average length smaller than Code II. A code is *compact* (for a given source) if its average length is less than or equal to the average length of all other prefix condition codes for the same source and the same code alphabet. According to this definition, Code II is compact for the source S. Although it may be easy to use an exhaustive search to find compact codes for sources with a small alphabet size, it is impractical to use such a scheme for large alphabets. The problem of constructing compact codes for any source will be considered in the section on Huffman coding.

3.1 Code Efficiency and Source Extensions

Although Code II is compact for S, its average length is still far greater than $H(S)$. Defining the *code efficiency* as the ratio

$$\eta = \frac{H(S)}{\overline{L}}, \tag{3.3}$$

---

[1]One may ask why we are not choosing all the codeword lengths as the largest integer smaller than $\log p(s_i)$ to further reduce the average length of the code. It turns out that a necessary and sufficient condition for constructing a prefix condition code with certain codeword lengths is that the lengths $l(s_i)$ satisfy a constraint known as the Kraft inequality $\sum_i 2^{-l(s_i)} \leq 1$, which the aforementioned construction does not.

the efficiency of Code II turns out to be 0.93. To achieve the performance stated in the noiseless coding theorem, one should encode the extensions of the source instead of the individual source symbols. Consider the second extension of S, S^2, which consists of 16 symbols formed as pairs of the symbols from the source S. Table 3.2 contains the source symbols with their corresponding probabilities and the compact code used to encode these symbols. The average length of the code is 2.86 bits per extended source symbol, which translates into 1.43 bits per original source symbol. This results in an efficiency of 0.98. The efficiency can be further improved by encoding even higher extensions of the source. Of course, the price paid is the complexity of encoding a larger symbol set.

Symbol	Probability	Word Length	Codeword
$s_1 s_1$	0.3600	1	0
$s_1 s_2$	0.1800	3	111
$s_1 s_3$	0.0300	5	10100
$s_1 s_4$	0.0300	5	10000
$s_2 s_1$	0.1800	3	110
$s_2 s_2$	0.0900	4	1011
$s_2 s_3$	0.0150	6	100010
$s_2 s_4$	0.0150	6	101010
$s_3 s_1$	0.0300	5	10011
$s_3 s_2$	0.0150	6	100011
$s_3 s_3$	0.0025	9	101011001
$s_3 s_4$	0.0025	9	101011000
$s_4 s_1$	0.0300	5	10010
$s_4 s_2$	0.0150	7	1010111
$s_4 s_3$	0.0025	9	101011011
$s_4 s_4$	0.0025	9	101011010

Table 3.2: Variable-length code for the 2nd extension of S.

3.2 Huffman Codes

A general method for constructing compact codes is due to Huffman [1] and is based on the following two principles:

- Consider a source with an alphabet of size α. By combining the two least probable symbols of this source, a new source with $\alpha - 1$ symbols is formed. Suppose that the codewords for this reduced source are known. It can be shown that the codewords for the original source are identical to the reduced source codewords for all symbols that have not been combined. Futhermore, the codewords for the two least probable symbols of the original source are formed by appending (to the right) '0' or '1' to the codeword corresponding to the combined symbol in the reduced source.

- The Huffman code for a source with only two symbols consists of the trivial codewords '0' and '1'.

Thus, to construct the Huffman code for a source S, the original source is repeatedly reduced by combining the two least probable symbols at each stage until a source with only two symbols is obtained. The Huffman code for this reduced source is known ('0' and '1'). Then, the codewords for the previous reduced stage are found by appending a '0' or '1' to the codeword corresponding to the two least probable symbols. This process is continued until the Huffman code for the original source is found. Figure 3.1a shows an example of the reduction process for a source with five symbols with probabilities 0.4, 0.2, 0.15, 0.15, and 0.10. For convenience, the source symbols are arranged in the order of decreasing probability. Figure 3.1b shows the codeword construction process for the sequence of reduced sources. The resulting Huffman code is $\{1, 000, 001, 010, 011\}$ with an average length of 2.20 bits/symbol. In comparison, the entropy of the source is 2.15 bits/symbol. For this example, applying the *ad hoc* method used to construct Code II in Table 3.1 results in the variable-length code $\{0, 10, 110, 1110, 1111\}$, which has an average length of 2.25 bits/symbol. The *ad hoc* method does not result in a compact code in this case.

3.3 Modified Huffman Codes

Frequently, most of the symbols in a large symbol set have very small probabilities. These symbols would take a disproportionately large share of the codeword memory since the codeword length for each symbol is roughly proportional to its information content, $-\log p(s_i)$. It is advantageous to lump the less probable symbols into a symbol called 'ELSE' and design a Huffman code for the reduced symbol set including the ELSE symbol [2]. This procedure is known as the *modified Huffman code*. Whenever a symbol belonging to the ELSE category needs to be encoded, the encoder transmits the codeword for ELSE followed by extra bits needed to identify the actual message within the ELSE category. If the symbols in the ELSE group have a small probability, the loss in coding efficiency (increase in average bit rate) will be very small while the storage requirements and the decoding complexity are substantially reduced.

One example of a sophisticated utilization of the above concept is the Group

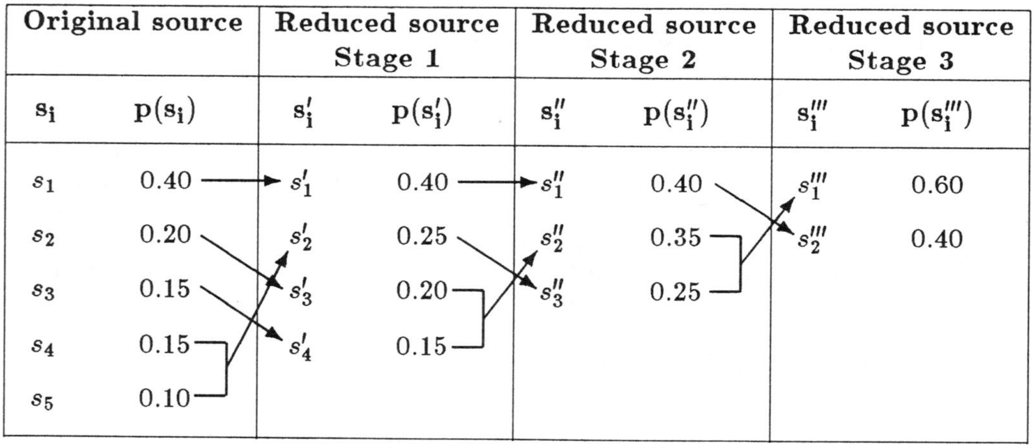

Original source		Reduced source Stage 1		Reduced source Stage 2		Reduced source Stage 3	
s_i	$p(s_i)$	s_i'	$p(s_i')$	s_i''	$p(s_i'')$	s_i'''	$p(s_i''')$
s_1	0.40	s_1'	0.40	s_1''	0.40	s_1'''	0.60
s_2	0.20	s_2'	0.25	s_2''	0.35	s_2'''	0.40
s_3	0.15	s_3'	0.20	s_3''	0.25		
s_4	0.15	s_4'	0.15				
s_5	0.10						

a) Source reduction process

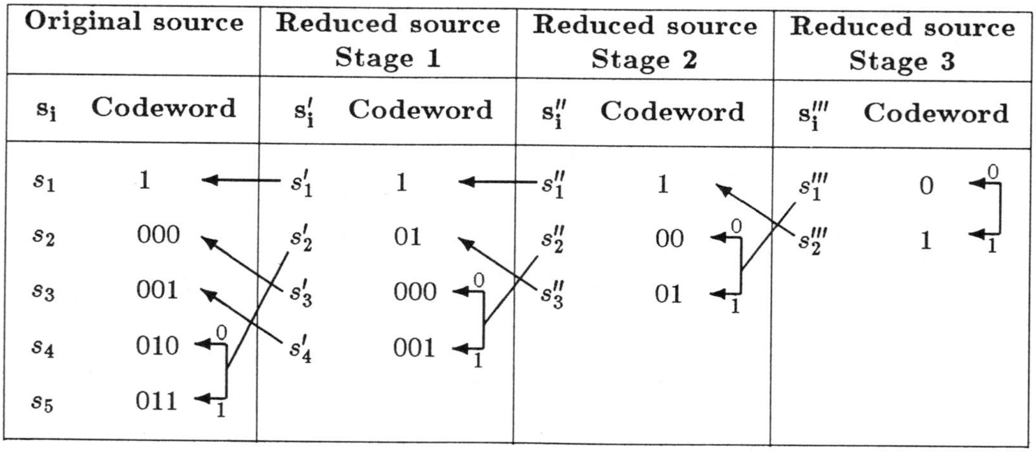

Original source		Reduced source Stage 1		Reduced source Stage 2		Reduced source Stage 3	
s_i	Codeword	s_i'	Codeword	s_i''	Codeword	s_i'''	Codeword
s_1	1	s_1'	1	s_1''	1	s_1'''	0
s_2	000	s_2'	01	s_2''	00	s_2'''	1
s_3	001	s_3'	000	s_3''	01		
s_4	010	s_4'	001				
s_5	011						

b) Codeword construction process

Figure 3.1: Huffman code generation.

3 international digital facsimile coding standards [3]. In this coding scheme, each binary image scan line is regarded as a sequence of alternating black and white runs which are encoded with separate variable-length code tables. A run is merely the number of times a particular value occurs consecutively along a scan line. Each run can potentially extend over a full scan line, which is 1728 pixels for this standard, and therefore each Huffman table should consist of 1728 entries. However, the Huffman table is greatly simplified by taking advantage of the fact that the longer runs are highly improbable. The first 64 entries in the table represent the Huffman codes for runs of 0 to 63 and are used to directly encode those runs. All other runs are represented as $64N + M$, where N is an integer between 1 and 27. The next 27 entries (entries 64 to 90) of the Huffman table are the codewords for the value of N. The value of M for these runs is then encoded using the first 64 entries. For example, a run of 213 is decomposed into $N = 3$ and $M = 21$, and its Huffman code consists of the entry 67 (64 + 3) followed by the entry 21 of the table. This process significantly simplifies the search required for decoding.

3.4   Limitations of Huffman Coding

In the previous sections, we saw how Huffman coding can encode source symbols with an average bit rate arbitrarily close to the source entropy. Although Huffman coding is a viable source coding technique, it suffers from several fundamental limitations.

One limitation arises because the ideal binary codeword length for a source symbol s_i from a DMS is $-\log_2 p(s_i)$. Since codeword lengths must be integers, this condition is met exactly only when the source symbol probabilities are negative powers of two, e.g., 1/2, 1/4, 1/8, etc. If the symbol probabilities significantly deviate from this ideal situation, direct encoding of the individual source symbols can result in poor code efficiency. For example, consider a source that has one symbol whose probability of occurrence is near 1, and hence all other symbols have low probabilities. Since the shortest possible codeword length is one, the bit rate for this source will be approximately 1 bit/symbol even though its entropy is significantly less than this. A special case of this situation occurs with binary sources since the Huffman codewords for '0' and '1' are '0' and '1'. The resulting bit rate is always 1 bit/symbol, regardless of the symbol probabilities. This bit rate matches the entropy of the binary source only if '0' and '1' occur with equal probability. To improve the coding efficiency under these conditions, we can encode the symbols of an extended source rather than the original source, but convergence to the source entropy may be slow. Also, since the number of entries in the Huffman code table grows exponentially with the block size, it may be necessary to settle for an inefficient code to avoid excessive implementation complexity.

The implementation complexity is further aggravated when Huffman coding is used to encode sequences generated by a Markov source. In general, for each state of the Markov source, the conditional probability distribution of the next symbol is different. Consequently, to encode the source at a rate near its entropy, a separate Huffman table is needed for each state. Even if a separate codebook is used for each state, the coding efficiency may still be low if the symbol probabilities deviate from the ideal case as discussed before. An alternative to using multiple codebooks is to use a single codebook and encode the adjoint of an extended source, that is, use memoryless block coding. However, for H_N, the entropy per original source symbol of the adjoint source, to reasonably approach H, the entropy of the Markov source (Eq. (2.17)), the block size typically must be large, which again makes the implementation impractical.

Another limitation is that Huffman coding cannot efficiently adapt to changing source statistics, and in fact, the use of a preset Huffman code with different sources may actually result in data expansion. A well-known example is when digitally halftoned images are compressed with the CCITT international digital facsimile data compression standard [3]. As much as a 50% data expansion can occur due to the fact that the CCITT algorithm uses predefined Huffman tables based on the statistics of binary texts and documents which are significantly different from the statistics of digital halftones. In order to provide adaptivity, Huffman coding is often implemented as a two-pass algorithm; the first pass gathers the symbol statistics and generates the codebook, and the second pass encodes the data. This approach works well when the symbol probabilities are constant within a given image. In many situations, however, the symbol probabilities change throughout an image, and the use of a fixed (static) Huffman code can severely affect the coding performance. Dynamic Huffman coding schemes exist [4-6] where the codewords are adaptively adjusted during the encoding and the decoding process, but their implementations are quite complex.

In the next section, we examine another variable-length coding strategy, known as arithmetic coding [7,8]. Although it is more complex than Huffman coding, arithmetic coding can overcome the limitations of Huffman coding.

3.5   Arithmetic Coding

To achieve a reasonable coding efficiency with Huffman coding, the sequence generated by the source is generally divided into blocks, and each block is assigned a variable-length codeword. At the decoder, the received sequence is parsed into variable-length blocks corresponding to the individual codewords. There is a one-to-one correspondence between the codeword blocks and the source sequence blocks. In comparison, arithmetic coding is a non-block code (also known as tree code), where a codeword is assigned to the entire input sequence s_m of length m symbols. In arithmetic coding, slightly different source sequences can result in significantly different code sequences. The codeword length approximately equals $-\log_2 p(\mathbf{s}_m)$, where $p(\mathbf{s}_m)$ is the probability of the source sequence $\mathbf{s}_m$. To understand the fundamental concepts of arithmetic coding, we first describe a computationally impractical version of that due to Elias [9,10] and then elaborate on the modifications required to render a practical technique. For simplicity, we will describe the process for a binary source, but the discussion applies to multisymbol sources as well.

Consider encoding a sequence of binary symbols, $\mathbf{s}_m$, generated by a DMS. Let p denote the probability of occurrence of a '0' and $q = 1 - p$ denote the probability of occurrence of a '1' in this sequence. Let us denote by I the half-open interval $[0, 1)$. Since the sum of $p(\mathbf{s}_m)$ over all the 2^m possible source sequences of length m is one, it is possible to assign a subinterval $I_l, l = 1, 2, \cdots, 2^m$, within I, to each source sequence $\mathbf{s}_m$, such that the length of I_l is equal to $p(\mathbf{s}_m)$ and the subintervals are nonoverlapping.

In the Elias code, this subinterval assignment is accomplished in the following manner. The interval I is first partitioned into two subintervals $[0, p)$ and $[p, 1)$ as in Fig. 3.2a. The subinterval $[0, p)$ is chosen if the first symbol in the sequence is a '0', and the subinterval $[p, 1)$ is chosen if it is a '1'. Then, each subinterval is further partitioned into two subintervals in a similar fashion. For the subinterval $[0, p)$, this partitioning results in two subintervals, $[0, p^2)$, $[p^2, p)$, and for the subinterval $[p, 1)$, it results in $[p, 2p - p^2)$ and $[2p - p^2, 1)$ as depicted in Fig. 3.2b. Together with the first symbol, the second symbol in the sequence is used to specify one of these subintervals. For example, the source sequence '01' corresponds to the subinterval $[p^2, p)$. Let us denote the subinterval specified after $j - 1$ binary source symbols by $[L^{(j-1)}, R^{(j-1)})$, where L stands for the left endpoint and R for the right endpoint. According to the above procedure, if the next symbol is a '0', a new subinterval $[L^{(j)}, R^{(j)})$ is specified, where

$$L^{(j)} = L^{(j-1)} \tag{3.4}$$

$$R^{(j)} = L^{(j-1)} + p(R^{(j-1)} - L^{(j-1)}), \tag{3.5}$$

and if it is a '1',

$$L^{(j)} = L^{(j-1)} + p(R^{(j-1)} - L^{(j-1)}) \tag{3.6}$$

$$R^{(j)} = R^{(j-1)}. \tag{3.7}$$

For any sequence, it can be shown that the subinterval generated by this method has a width equal to the probability of the sequence. Furthermore, the subintervals produced by all the possible sequences of length m are nonoverlapping, and their union completely covers the interval I.

Once the subinterval $[L_l, R_l)$, $(l = 1, 2, \cdots, 2^m)$, corresponding to a certain source sequence $\mathbf{s}_m$, has been identified, a codeword for $\mathbf{s}_m$ can be constructed by expanding the subinterval beginning point, L_l, in binary form and retaining only the $n_l = \lceil -\log_2 p(\mathbf{s}_m) \rceil$ bits after the decimal

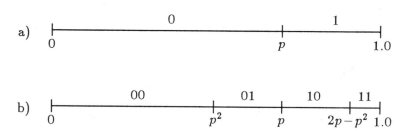

Figure 3.2: Elias code partitioning.

point. By expanding the point in binary form, we mean, for example, $0.8125 = 1/2 + 1/4 + 1/16 \rightarrow 0.1101$. The reason the codewords can be constructed in this manner is that the beginning point of each subinterval is separated from the beginning point of its nearest right-hand neighbor by the subinterval width $p(\mathbf{s}_m)$, where

$$p(\mathbf{s}_m) \geq 2^{-n_l}. \tag{3.8}$$

As a result, the first n_l bits of the binary expansions of the two adjacent subintervals cannot be identical, and only n_l bits are required to uniquely specify the subinterval I_l (and hence to specify the source sequence $\mathbf{s}_m$). This encoding operation has a sliding structure; as a few source symbols enter the encoder, a few code symbols leave the decoder. For example, as soon as the encoder has received enough source symbols to determine if I_l belongs to the interval $[0, 0.5)$ or to $[0.5, 1)$, it knows whether the first output bit is a '0' or a '1'. Additional codeword bits are generated as I_l becomes more finely specified. In a similar manner, the decoder can also start decoding after receiving only a few code symbols. Note that there is no one-to-one correspondence between the codeword bits and blocks of input sequence bits as is the case in Huffman coding.

The previous discussion was based on the assumption that the source is memoryless, but it can easily be extended to a Markov source. Consider the subinterval specified after $j - 1$ source symbols. The next partitioning is based on the value of p for the jth symbol. In the case of a Markov source, this value is not a constant and is determined by the previously encoded source symbols, i.e, by the state of the Markov source. Equations (3.5) and (3.6) can be easily extended to a Markov source by using $p^{(j)}$ instead of p, where $p^{(j)}$ denotes the dependence of p on the position of the symbol within the source sequence. The decoder, as it decodes each symbol, constructs the state corresponding to the next symbol, and uses the appropriate $p^{(j)}$ value to decode the next symbol.

The major implementation problem of the Elias code is the precision required to carry out the subinterval computations. As the length of the source sequence increases, the length of the subinterval specified by the sequence decreases, and more bits are required to precisely identify the subinterval. Practical implementations of arithmetic coding address this problem by introducing a scaling (renormalization) strategy and a rounding strategy [11-13]. The scaling strategy magnifies each subinterval prior to partitioning so that its length is always close to 1. The rounding strategy uses b-bit (e.g., 16-bit) finite-precision arithmetic to measure the subinterval and perform the partitioning. To be able to represent all the nonzero symbol probabilities, the value of b should be chosen such that the smallest symbol probability is always larger than 2^{-b}. Generally, a larger b results in less quantization and renders a more efficient code. It is outside the scope of this book to discuss the actual implementation issues concerning the various arithmetic coding strategies, and instead, we have tried to present the underlying concept by studying the Elias code. In the next section, we briefly examine a particular implementation of a binary arithmetic coder, known as the Q-coder [14], which has been developed by IBM. Without explaining the inner workings of the Q-coder, we describe how it can be used to overcome the problems associated with Huffman encoding.

3.5.1 The IBM Q-coder

The IBM Q-coder is a form of *adaptive binary* arithmetic coding aimed at simplifying software and hardware implementations [15]. The major features of the Q-coder are summarized below:

- It can only encode binary sequences. For nonbinary sources, a binary decision tree must be constructed to characterize the source symbols. The result of each binary decision can then be encoded by the Q-coder. For more detail on the construction of binary decision trees, the reader is referred to the section on Arithmetic Encoding of Differential Images in Chapter 7: Lossless Predictive Coding.

- It uses a 12-bit register to implement the coding operation, but instead of allowing 2^{12} different values for the probability of the symbol to be encoded, a table with only 30 quantized values for the probability of the less probable symbol (LPS) is used [16]. The table was empirically determined and is a trade-off among many factors. Also, approximations are made which allow the interval partitioning based on the probabilities to be approximated by subtractions or table look-ups, rather than requiring multiplications.

- Unlike Huffman coding, it does not require an estimate of the probability of the symbols to be encoded; it arrives at a robust probability estimate for a source symbol after encoding it only a few times [17]. For example, when encoding a binary Markov source, the value of p in each state can be initialized to 0.50. Once a certain state has been visited several times, the Q-coder arrives at a fairly accurate (within the quantization noise of the 30 allowable values) estimate of p (or $q = 1 - p$, whichever is smaller) for that state. By updating the quantized probability estimate in any subsequent visits, the Q-coder can easily cope with changes in the source statistics. The probability estimation technique is based on the interval renormalization that is a necessary part of the finite-precision arithmetic coding process, and as a result, it adds little to the complexity.

- When the Q-coder is used to encode a *stationary* binary DMS (single-context encoding), its output bit rate is about 5 to 6% above the source entropy, depending on the value of p. This is due partly to the restricted set of available probability estimates, partly to fluctuations in the probability estimation process, and partly to the approximations used in the interval partitioning process [17]. Multiple-context encoding (as for stationary Markov sources) results in an additional 1% inefficiency on the average. However, since the Q-coder is able to track the symbol probabilities fairly well for *nonstationary* sources, its performance in coding real images is extremely good.

As noted, the sequence of source symbols must be translated into a binary sequence when using the Q-coder. Since the probability of each binary symbol may depend on its neighbors, one should define a number of distinct conditioning states for which a probability estimate needs to be maintained. Each conditioning state is referred to as a *context*. For example, when dealing with a Markov source, one may define a separate context for each state of the Markov source, but it is important to realize that a context does not always correspond to an individual state of the Markov source. For example, a few states with similar values of p may be merged under the same context. Furthermore, quantities other than neighboring pixel values (local gradients, for example) may be used to define the contexts in image coding.

Each context uses a 6-bit storage bin in the Q-coder, where one bit indicates the LPS within that context and five bits denote the probability estimate of the LPS in that context. The input to the Q-coder is the binary source symbol along with its 6-bit context value. In the process of encoding the source symbol, the probability estimate within that context is updated and stored in the corresponding context bin. The encoding of a certain source symbol may result in no output bits or several output bits, depending on the likelihood of the symbol in that particular context.

Chapter 4

Entropy Estimation and Lossless Compression

A frequently asked question is how much lossless compression can be achieved for a given image. In light of the noiseless source coding theorem, we know that the bit rate can be made arbitrarily close to the entropy of the source that generated the image. However, a fundamental problem is determining that entropy.

An obvious approach to estimating the entropy is to characterize the source using a certain model and then find the entropy with respect to that model. Accurate source modeling is essential to any compression scheme since the performance bounds are established by the entropy with respect to that model. The effectiveness of a model is determined by how accurately it predicts the symbol probabilities. With natural information-generating sources such as speech and images, the more complex models, which are capable of accounting for the structure present in such sources, result in lower entropies and higher compression. The real challenge with this approach lies in approximating the source structure as close as possible while keeping the complexity of the model (the number of parameters) to a minimum.

Another approach to estimating the entropy is to segment the image into blocks of size N and use the frequency of occurrence of each block as a measure of its probability. The entropy per original source symbol of the adjoint source formed in this way would approach the entropy of the original source as the block size goes to infinity. Unfortunately, the convergence to the true entropy is slow and one needs to consider large values of N. Since there are 256^N possible values for each N-pixel block with an 8-bit image, the required computational resources would run scarce even for small values of N.

To illustrate the problem of entropy estimation for an actual source, we will consider an example involving the English language. We first use successively more complex source models to represent the structure of the English language and find the corresponding entropies. Then, we discuss an interesting method proposed by Shannon for estimating the entropy of the English language. Finally, we consider the extension of this technique to estimating the entropies of natural images.

4.1   Structure and Entropy of the English Language

In this example, which has been outlined in detail in [9], we try to model a source which generates a message composed of English words. For simplicity, we restrict ourselves to a set of 27 symbols consisting of the 26 letters of the English alphabet and a space which we denote by "*". The simplest model for a source using such an alphabet is a DMS with equiprobable symbols, i.e., $p(s_i) = 1/27$, for $i = 1, ..., 27$. The entropy of this source is

$$H(S) = \log_2(27) = 4.75 \quad \text{bits/symbol}.$$

A typical text generated by such a model would be:

ZEWRTZYNSADXESYJRQY*WGECIJJ*OBVKRBQPOZBYMB
UAWVLBTQCNIKFMP*KMVUUGBSAXHLHSIE*M.

This model does not reflect any of the structure contained in the English language. As a result, its entropy (uncertainty) is high, and a coding scheme based on this model cannot reduce the redundancy present in the language.

A better model can be constructed by employing the actual probabilities of the symbols as given in Table 4.1. These probabilities were generated by examining typical English text.

A DMS based on such symbol probabilities has an entropy

$$H(S) = \sum_S p(s_i) \log_2 \left(\frac{1}{p(s_i)} \right) = 4.03 \quad \text{bits/symbol}.$$

A typical text generated by such a model would be:

AI*NGAE**ITF*NNR*ASAEV*OIE*BAINTHA*HYROO*POE
R*SETRYGAIETRWCO**EHDUARU*EU*C*FT*NSREM*DI
Y*EESE**F*O*SRIS*R**UNNAS.

Although the above text hardly qualifies as good English, it does reflect some of the structure of the language. For example, the words generated

Symbol	Probability	Symbol	Probability
Space	0.1859	N	0.0574
A	0.0642	O	0.0632
B	0.0127	P	0.0152
C	0.0218	Q	0.0008
D	0.0317	R	0.0484
E	0.1031	S	0.0514
F	0.0208	T	0.0796
G	0.0152	U	0.0228
H	0.0467	V	0.0083
I	0.0575	W	0.0175
J	0.0008	X	0.0013
K	0.0049	Y	0.0164
L	0.0321	Z	0.0005
M	0.0198		

Table 4.1: Probability of the letters in the English alphabet.

by this model contain a more realistic proportion of vowels and consonants than the previous model. The main drawback of this model is that it does not take into account any of the dependence among the different letters. In an actual text, a space would never be followed by another space, and the letter Q would almost invariably be followed by the letter U.

A simple model that can accommodate this dependence of successive symbols is a first-order Markov source with the appropriate conditional probabilities. To model such a source, we need 27 probability tables similar in size to Table 4.1, one for each state of the Markov source determined by the preceding letter. These probabilities are taken from [18]. The entropy of this first-order Markov model is

$$H(S) = \sum_S \sum_S p(s_i, s_j) \log_2\left(\frac{1}{p(s_i|s_j)}\right) = 3.32 \quad \text{bits/symbol.}$$

A typical text generated by such a model would be:

URTESHETHING∗AD∗E∗AT∗FOULE∗ITHALIORT∗WACT∗D
∗STE∗MINTSAN∗OLINS∗TWID∗OULY∗TE∗THIGHE∗CO∗YS
∗TH∗HR∗UPAVIDE∗PAD∗CTAVED.

We can further improve upon our model by considering a second-order Markov source. Such a model would involve 729 (27×27) probability tables, one for each combination of the previous two letters. The entropy of the

English language with respect to this model is [19]

$$H(S) = \sum_S \sum_S \sum_S p(s_i, s_j, s_k) \log_2 \left(\frac{1}{p(s_i|s_j, s_k)} \right) = 3.1 \quad \text{bits/symbol.}$$

A typical text generated by such a model would be:

IANKS*CAN*OU*ANG*RLER*THATTED*OF*TO*SHOR*OF
*TO*HAVEMEM*A*I*MAND*AND*BUT*WHISSITABLY*TH
ERVEREER*EIGHTS*TAKILLIS*TA.

We can reasonably claim that one would have little trouble identifying this sequence as an approximation to English instead of, say, French. However, it is still far from capturing the full structure present in the English language. If we encode an English text based on this model, we expect to achieve a bit rate close to 3.1 bits/symbol, as compared to 4.75 bits/symbol resulting from our initial DMS model. We can obtain successively better estimates of the entropy of the English language by increasing the order of the Markov source. Unfortunately, the size of the model parameters grows exponentially, and the convergence to the true entropy of the source is slow. An accompanying problem is that the encoding scheme needed to achieve a bit rate close to the entropy of the model would soon become impractical. Using a different technique, Shannon [19] has estimated that the entropy of the English language is between 0.6 and 1.3 bits/symbol. This technique is described in the next section.

4.2   Predictability and Entropy of the English Language

To estimate the entropy of the English language, Shannon [19] exploited the fact that anyone speaking a language implicitly possesses an enormous knowledge of the language. He found upper and lower bounds to the entropy of printed English by eliciting knowledge of the conditional probability distribution of the symbols from a subject through the use of a guessing game. The experiment proceeded as follows: A subject was shown $N-1$ consecutive symbols of an unfamiliar text, and was asked to guess the next letter in the passage. Guesses continued until the correct letter was selected. This guessing process ranks the possible choices in decreasing order of conditional probability based on the subject's knowledge of the English language. The experiment was repeated n times. Denoting by q_i^N the number of times the subject required i guesses to discover the correct letter *given* the previous $N-1$ letters, Shannon showed that the entropy of the text is bounded by

$$\sum_{i=1}^{27} i \left(\frac{q_i^N}{n} - \frac{q_{i+1}^N}{n} \right) \log_2 i \leq H(S) \leq - \sum_{i=1}^{27} \frac{q_i^N}{n} \log_2 \left(\frac{q_i^N}{n} \right). \qquad (4.1)$$

In his experiment, one hundred samples of English text were selected at random from a book, each a hundred letters in length ($N = 100$). Based on Eq. (4.1), Shannon arrived at an upper bound of 1.3 bits/symbol and a lower bound of 0.6 bits/symbol for written English. The upper bound is loose for three reasons: (1) N is finite (only $N \to \infty$ reflects the complete information regarding the past); (2) q_i^N is determined by a mixture of q_i^N conditioned on the past; e.g., the probability of getting the right answer in the third guess was different in all those cases when the subject had to make three guesses; and (3) the sample size is finite (the experiment must be repeated many times before q_i^N/n converges to its mean value). Other experiments have been performed to estimate the entropy of the English language, and an extensive bibliography appears in [20]. It should be noted that the entropies associated with different authors are different. Similarly, the entropy of a given text with respect to different human subjects also varies since each subject may possess a different degree of knowledge of the language.

4.3   Predictability and Entropy of Natural Images

Kersten [21] used a procedure similar to Shannon's guessing experiment to estimate the entropy and redundancy of natural images. In his study, eight pictures, ranging from a busy scene of foliage to a less detailed picture of a face, were sampled at 128×128 pixels and were digitized to 4 bits (16 gray levels or symbols). Before the observer was allowed to see the pictures, a predetermined fraction of the pixels was deleted (most data were collected with 1% deletion). The observer was asked to set the level of a deleted pixel (which would blink) to its original value. The observer would ask the computer to paint the pixel with various gray levels from the palette shown beneath the picture until he was satisfied with his choice. If the choice was right, the observer went on to the next pixel. If the choice was wrong, the observer kept guessing until it was correct. A marker was placed on the palette indicating wrong choices, so that the observer would not pick those again. The experiment was repeated 100 times, and a histogram of the number of guesses was formed. The redundancy of an image was defined as 1 minus the ratio of the entropy to the actual number of bits used to represent the image (in this case, 4 bits). Using Shannon's upper and lower entropy bounds, it was concluded that for the eight images used in the experiment, the redundancy ranged from 46%, for the busiest picture, to 74%, for a picture of a face.

Great caution should be exercised in generalizing these results to images that have been generated under different conditions. In general, many factors contribute to the redundancy (and thus compressibility) of an image. One factor is the quantization step used in digitizing the image. The images in this experiment were quantized to 4 bits; most consumer imagery uses 8 bits. As we shall see later, the less significant bits display very little structure, and as a result, finer quantization reduces the redundancy of an image. Another important factor is the level of the noise in an image. Noise, by its very nature, is unpredictable and cannot be compressed. A third factor is the resolution used to scan the image. In general, higher resolution results in more dependence among pixels and increases the redundancy.

Chapter 5

Rate-Distortion Theory and Lossy Compression

The performance bound on the encoding rate of an information source, as defined by the source entropy, pertains only to the lossless encoding of the data. In many practical situations, a certain degree of irreversible image degradation can be tolerated. This level of degradation is usually controlled by the user by adjusting a set of parameters, e.g., quantization intervals. A relevant question is: What is the minimum bit rate required to encode a source while keeping the resulting degradation below a certain level? This fundamental question is addressed by a branch of information theory known as *rate-distortion theory* [22]. Rate-distortion theory establishes theoretical performance bounds for lossy data compression according to a fidelity criterion. For a broad class of distortion measures and source models, the theory provides a *rate-distortion function* $R(D)$ that has the following properties:

- For any given level of distortion D, it is possible to find a coding scheme with rate arbitrarily close to $R(D)$ and average distortion arbitrarily close to D.

- It is impossible to find a code that achieves reproduction with distortion D (or better) at a rate below $R(D)$.

It can be shown that $R(D)$ is a convex $\cup$, continuous, and strictly decreasing function of D. Figure 5.1 shows a typical rate-distortion function for a discrete source with a finite alphabet. The minimum rate required for distortion-free compression of the source is the value of R at $D = 0$ and is less than or equal to the source entropy, depending on the distortion measure. Also shown is the hypothetical performance of a high-complexity encoder and a low-complexity encoder relative to the $R(D)$ bound. In general,

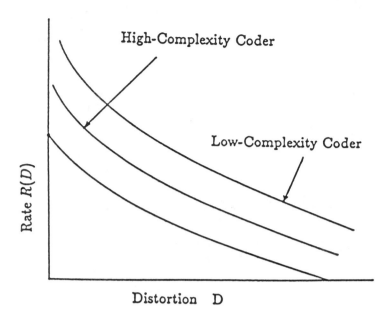

Figure 5.1: Example of a rate-distortion curve and typical encoder performance.

a more sophisticated coding scheme that better models the source statistics achieves a performance closer to the $R(D)$ bound.

To characterize the function $R(D)$, one needs a source model and a distortion criterion. The problem becomes mathematically tractable if the source is modeled as a DMS and the distortion measure is *context-free* with a simple form. A context-free measure, also known as single-letter distortion, implies that the distortion is a function of the original symbol and its reproduced value and does not depend on the other terms in the sequence of source symbols and their reproductions. Under these assumptions, closed-form solutions have been found for some source distributions using a mean-square-error or mean-absolute-error distortion criterion [23]. For those distributions where a closed-form solution does not exist, a numerical solution can be found by using an iterative algorithm suggested by Blahut [24]. Unfortunately, the above results are of little utility to images. Natural imagery is highly correlated and cannot be adequately modeled by a DMS. Also, in most applications, the compressed image is viewed by a human subject, and for each pixel, the perceived distortion is a complex function of that pixel value *and* the surrounding pixel values. This limits the utility of context-free distortion measures. Furthermore, even in the simplest cases, the implementation of the optimal coding scheme which achieves the theoretical bound might be very complex. Although the available theoretical results are limited for sources with memory, one important case where a solution exists is for a Gaussian source with a weighted quadratic-error distortion measure

[25]. By modeling an image as a two-dimensional Gauss-Markov source with a correlation coefficient close to one, the rate-distortion results may be employed to establish a reference performance. The determination of $R(D)$ for source models that accurately describe natural imagery and for distortion measures that correlate well with visual criteria remains an active research problem.

References

[1] D. A. Huffman, "A method for the construction of minimum redundancy codes," Proc. IRE, 40, 1098-1101 (1952).

[2] M. Hankamer, "A modified huffman procedure with reduced memory requirement," IEEE Trans. Commun., COM-27(6), 930-932 (1979).

[3] R. Hunter and A. H. Robinson, "International digital facsimile standards," Proc. IEEE, 68(7), 854-867, (1980).

[4] R. G. Gallager, "Variations on a theme by Huffman," IEEE Trans. Info. Theory, IT-24(6), 668-674 (1978).

[5] D. E. Knuth, "Dynamic Huffman coding," J. Algorithms, 6, 163-180 (1985).

[6] J. S. Vitter, "Design and analysis of dynamic Huffman coding," in *Proc. 26th Annual IEEE Symposium on Foundations of Computer Science,* Portland, Oregon, IEEE Computer Society, 293-302 (1985).

[7] G. G. Langdon, "An introduction to arithmetic coding," IBM J. Res. Dev., 28(2), 135-149 (1984).

[8] J. Rissanen and G. G. Langdon, "Arithmetic coding," IBM J. Res. Dev., 23(2), 149-162 (1979).

[9] N. Abramson, *Information Theory and Coding,* McGraw-Hill, New York (1963).

[10] R. E. Blahut, *Principles and Practice of Information Theory,* Addison-Wesley, Reading, MA (1987).

[11] C. B. Jones, "An efficient coding system for long source sequences," IEEE Trans. Info. Theory, IT-27(3), 280-291 (1981).

[12] I. H. Witten, R. M. Neal, and J. G. Cleary, "Arithmetic coding for data compression," Communications of ACM, 30(6), 520-540 (1987).

[13] G. G. Langdon and J. J. Rissanen, "Compression of black-white images with arithmetic coding," IEEE Trans. Commun., COM-29(6), 858-867 (1981).

[14] W. B. Pennebaker, J. L. Mitchell, G. G. Langdon, Jr., and R. B. Arps, "An overview of the basic principles of the Q-coder adaptive binary arithmetic coder," IBM J. Res. Dev., 32(6), 717-726 (1988).

[15] J. L. Mitchell and W. B. Pennebaker "Optimal hardware and software arithmetic coding procedures for the Q-coder," IBM J. Res. Dev., 32(6), 727-736 (1988).

[16] J. L. Mitchell and W. B. Pennebaker "Software implementations of the Q-coder," IBM J. Res. Dev., 32(6), 753-774 (1988).

[17] W. B. Pennebaker and J. L. Mitchell, "Probability estimation for the Q-coder," IBM J. Res. Dev., 32(6), 737-752 (1988).

[18] F. Pratt, *Secret and Urgent*, Doubleday & Company, Inc., Garden City, NY (1942).

[19] C. E. Shannon, "Prediction and entropy of printed English," Bell Syst. Tech. J., 30, 50-64 (1951).

[20] T. M. Cover and R. C. King, "A convergent gambling estimate of the entropy of English," IEEE Trans. Info. Theory, IT-24(4), 413-421 (1978).

[21] D. Kersten, "Predictability and redundancy of natural images," J. Opt. Soc. Am. A, 4(12), 2395-2400 (1987).

[22] T. Berger, *Rate Distortion Theory*, Prentice-Hall, Engelwood Cliffs, NJ (1971).

[23] H. Tan and K. Yao, "Evaluation of rate distortion functions for a class of independent identically distributed sources under an absolute magnitude criterion," IEEE Trans. Info. Theory, IT-21, 59-63 (1975).

[24] R. Blahut, "Computation of channel capacity and rate distortion functions," IEEE Trans. Info. Theory, IT-18(4), 460-473 (1972).

[25] L. D. Davisson, "Rate-distortion theory and application," Proc. IEEE, 60(7), 800-808 (1972).

Part III

Lossless Compression
Techniques

Introduction

Some image compression applications require the reconstructed image to be *lossless*, i.e., numerically identical to the original on a pixel-by-pixel basis. An example is in medical imaging where compressing digital radiographs with a lossy scheme (and hence introducing errors) may compromise diagnostic accuracy. As one might expect, the price to be paid for an error-free reconstruction is a much lower compression ratio as compared to lossy schemes.

Lossless techniques for binary images have been summarized in general survey articles [1,2]. For continuous-tone images, a number of different techniques based on such concepts as runlength encoding, bit plane processing, predictive coding, hierarchical transformation, and quadtree representations have appeared in the literature [3-14]. Recently, simple and efficient implementations of adaptive arithmetic coding such as the Q-coder [15] have further improved the performance of lossless techniques.

In the next three chapters, we examine three popular strategies for lossless coding of continuous-tone images, namely, bit plane encoding, lossless predictive coding, and lossy plus lossless residual encoding. The compression efficiency varies somewhat for the different techniques, but the choice of a particular approach is not determined strictly by the achievable bit rate. This is because each strategy offers certain features and aims at satisfying certain requirements that might exist in a particular environment.

Chapter 6

Bit Plane Encoding

Consider an $N \times N$ image in which each pixel value is represented by k bits. By selecting a single bit from the same position in the binary representation of each pixel, an $N \times N$ binary image called a *bit plane* can be formed [6]. For example, we can select the most significant bit of each pixel value to generate an $N \times N$ binary image representing the most significant bit plane. Repeating this process for the other bit positions, the original image can be decomposed into a set of k, $N \times N$ bit planes (numbered 0 for the least significant bit (LSB) plane through $k - 1$ for the most significant bit (MSB) plane). The motivation for this decomposition is that each bit plane can then be encoded efficiently using a lossless binary compression technique. Furthermore, in certain applications, the user may desire a low bit rate approximation to the original image before making the decision to proceed to a lossless mode. Since the more significant bit planes generally contain major structural information and are highly compressible, progressively reconstructing an image using the bit planes can be a viable technique for this purpose. This technique of *progressive transmission* is discussed in more detail in Chapter 14: Hierarchical Coding under Lossy Compression Techniques.

6.1 Gray Code

Bit plane encoding algorithms typically encode the bit planes independently and take advantage of the existence of large uniform areas (coherency) in each plane to achieve high compression. To this end, it is desirable to form the bit planes in such a way as to minimize their complexity, i.e., the transitions among the neighboring binary pixel values in each plane. Unfortunately, constructing the bit planes from the conventional binary representation of the pixel values does not achieve this purpose.

49

To see this, consider an 8-bit image whose pixel values randomly fluctuate between the code values 127 and 128. Although the entropy of this image is only 1 bit/pixel, independent encoding of the bit planes requires a total of 8 bits/pixel. This is because the binary representations of the integers 127 and 128 are 01111111 and 10000000, respectively. Since they differ at every bit position, the resulting bit planes lack coherence. Note that all of the bit planes in this example are completely correlated, and a scheme that *jointly* encodes the planes could take advantage of this correlation to achieve the 1 bit/pixel rate. However, since most schemes encode the bit planes independently to reduce the implementation complexity, it is necessary to find a method to increase their coherence. One simple approach is to form the bit planes based on the Gray code representation of the pixel values [16,17].

The Gray code is a method of mapping a set of numbers into a binary alphabet such that successive numerical changes result in a change of only one bit in the binary representation. Thus, when two neighboring pixels differ by one code value, only a single bit plane is affected. Figure 6.1 shows the binary code (BC) and the Gray code (GC) representations of the 4-bit numbers 0 to 15. The bit values of 0 and 1 are represented by the white and the black areas, respectively. It is seen that the MSB planes of the binary and the Gray codes are identical while, in general, the complexity (as measured by the number of transitions) of the lth Gray code bit plane is approximately the same as the complexity of the $(l + 1)$th binary bit plane.

The mapping rule from binary code to Gray code is as follows:

1. Starting with the MSB of the binary code representation, all 0's are left intact until a 1 is encountered.

2. The 1 is left intact, but all the following bits are complemented until a 0 is encountered.

3. The 0 is complemented, but all the following bits are left intact until a 1 is encountered.

4. Go to step 2.

The inverse mapping is

1. Starting from the MSB of the Gray code representation, all 0's are left intact until a 1 is encountered.

2. The 1 is left intact, but all the following bits are complemented until another 1 is encountered.

3. The 1 is complemented, but all the following bits are left intact until another 1 is encountered.

4. Go to step 2.

Figures 6.2 and 6.3 show the binary and the Gray code bit planes of the LENA image. BP 7 represents the MSB plane while BP 0 represents the LSB plane. These figures demonstrate that the complexity of the bit planes increases as one moves to the lower planes and that the complexity of the Gray code bit planes are always less than that of the corresponding binary bit planes. We now examine various methods of encoding the bit planes.

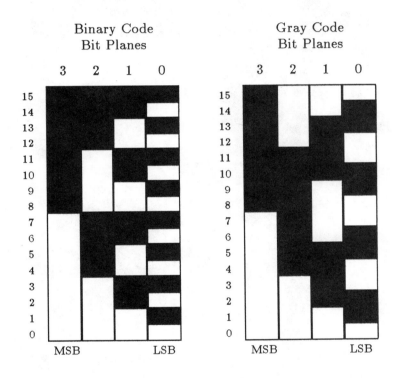

Figure 6.1: 4-bit binary and Gray codes.

6.2   Runlength Encoding of Bit Planes

The simplest method of encoding binary data where clusters of 0's and 1's occur frequently is runlength coding [18]. Both 1-D and 2-D runlength coding techniques are routinely used for the encoding of binary text and documents in the field of facsimile transmission. In runlength coding, a new message set is constructed based on the runs of 0's and 1's. In 1-D runlength coding, the runs of 0's and 1's are variable-length encoded using separate Huffman tables

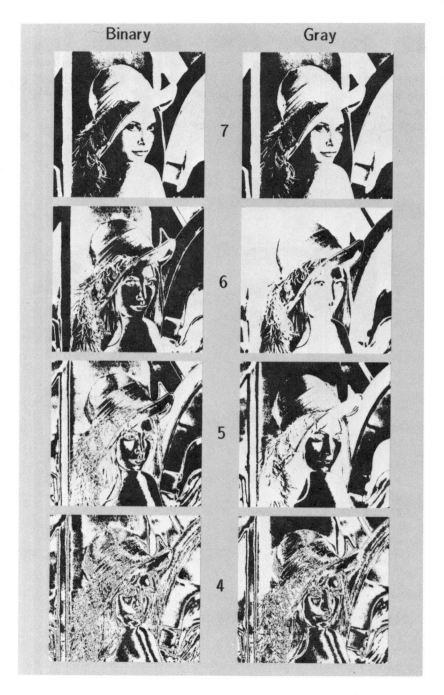

Figure 6.2: Binary and Gray code bit planes for LENA, (BP 7 through 4).

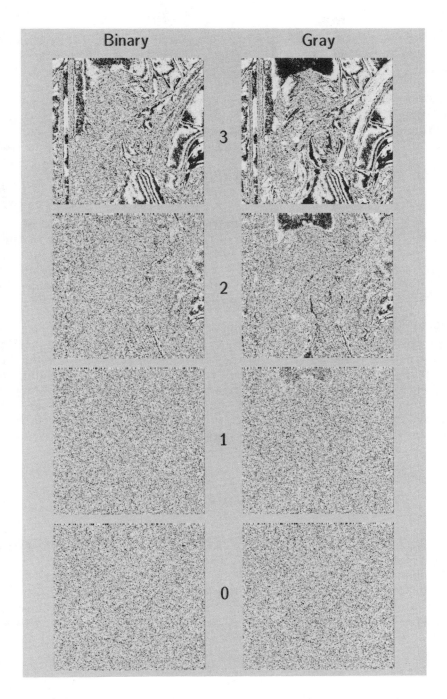

Figure 6.3: Binary and Gray code bit planes for LENA, (BP 3 through 0).

tailored to the statistics of each. Many variations exist for 2-D runlength encoding, but the basic idea is to encode the starting position of a run in the current line relative to the previous line. In general, 2-D runlength coding achieves higher compression ratios since it uses the vertical correlation in an image.

Table 6.1 summarizes the entropies in bits/pixel resulting from 1-D runlength encoding of the bit planes. The results for the binary code (BC) are listed in column 2, and the results for the Gray code (GC) are listed in column 3. The 1-D runlength entropy, H, is calculated according to

$$H = \frac{H_0 + H_1}{\bar{r}_0 + \bar{r}_1}, \tag{6.1}$$

where H_0 and H_1 are the entropies in bits/runlength symbol of the 0 and 1 runs, respectively, and $\bar{r}_0$ and $\bar{r}_1$ are the average runlengths of the 0's and 1's, respectively. It should be noted that the 1-D runlength entropy of each bit plane is a lower bound to the bit rate achievable by any encoding scheme that encodes the 1-D runs. In practice, a global Huffman code would probably be used, resulting in somewhat higher bit rates.

The entropy values for both the binary representation and the Gray code representation increase substantially as one moves from the MSB plane (BP 7) to the LSB plane (BP 0). This indicates that there is a lot of redundancy in the higher planes while the lower planes behave almost like random noise. Except for BP 7 where Gray and binary MSBs are identical, the Gray code entropies are generally smaller than the corresponding binary code entropies. In particular, the Gray code representation significantly outperforms the binary representation in the higher bit planes.

6.3   Arithmetic Encoding of Bit Planes

The application of an adaptive binary arithmetic coder such as the Q-coder to bit plane data is straightforward. The m neighboring pixels of the current pixel can be used to form a context, c, for encoding that pixel [19]. In this model, the image is assumed to have been generated by an mth-order Markov source where each state is determined by a certain combination of the m neighboring pixels. In general, m binary-valued pixels constitute 2^m states where each state is used to form a context.

The entropy of the mth-order Markov source can be computed if the stationary probabilities of the contexts, $p(c)$, $c = 1, 2, \cdots, 2^m$, and the conditional probabilities of a 0 in each context, $p(0|c)$, $c = 1, 2, \cdots, 2^m$, are known. A nonadaptive binary arithmetic coder that uses knowledge of $p(0|c)$ would encode the Markov source at a bit rate very close to its entropy. If an adaptive coder such as the Q-Coder is employed, the resulting bit rate may be

Bit Plane	1-D Runlength Entropy		7-pixel 2-D Q-Coder Bit Rate		7-pixel 3-D Q-Coder Bit Rate	
	BC	GC	BC	GC	BC	GC
LENA						
BP 7	0.274	0.274	0.144	0.144	0.144	0.144
BP 6	0.452	0.282	0.279	0.150	0.162	0.153
BP 5	0.614	0.390	0.450	0.235	0.263	0.237
BP 4	0.838	0.714	0.736	0.571	0.541	0.540
BP 3	0.965	0.908	0.955	0.860	0.753	0.788
BP 2	0.999	0.996	1.039	1.027	0.976	0.982
BP 1	1.000	1.000	1.043	1.042	1.040	1.039
BP 0	1.000	1.000	1.043	1.042	1.042	1.042
Total	6.142	5.564	5.689	5.071	4.921	4.925
BOOTS						
BP 7	0.292	0.292	0.187	0.187	0.187	0.187
BP 6	0.487	0.342	0.370	0.228	0.234	0.228
BP 5	0.690	0.565	0.607	0.454	0.479	0.445
BP 4	0.829	0.752	0.795	0.683	0.663	0.654
BP 3	0.915	0.883	0.933	0.877	0.836	0.840
BP 2	0.942	0.935	0.982	0.968	0.948	0.948
BP 1	0.945	0.945	0.986	0.986	0.981	0.981
BP 0	0.946	0.946	0.988	0.989	0.986	0.986
Total	6.046	5.660	5.848	5.372	5.316	5.269

Table 6.1: Runlength entropies and Q-coder bit rates for bit plane encoding.

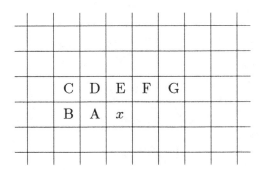

Figure 6.4: 7-pixel context configuration for Q-coded bit planes.

even lower than the entropy in certain cases. This is because the entropy calculation assumes a stationary Markov source model, i.e., $p(0|c)$ is fixed for each state, whereas the conditional probabilities may vary substantially from one area of the image to another. Since an adaptive coder updates the estimate of $p(0|c)$ every time that it visits a particular context, its knowledge of $p(0|c)$ is more accurate than a global estimate and is thus capable of encoding the source at a lower bit rate.

Figure 6.4 illustrates the neighboring 7-pixel (128 contexts) orientation used in [19] to encode the pixel x. The actual bit rates (not entropies) resulting from using this context model with the Q-coder to encode the binary and the Gray bit planes are given in columns 4 and 5 of Table 6.1. Since the 7-pixel context takes advantage of 2-D information, the resulting Q-coder bit rates are lower than the corresponding 1-D runlength entropies. Furthermore, the Gray code results in lower bit rates with the Q-coder than does the binary code. For example, the total bit rate required for the four most significant Gray code bit planes of LENA using the Q-coder is only 1.10 bits/pixel while the sum for the binary code using the Q-coder is 1.61 bits/pixel. In comparison, the sum of the 1-D runlength entropies of the same four bit planes is 1.66 bits/pixel for the Gray code and 2.18 bits/pixel for the binary code.

As seen from Table 6.1, each of the three least significant bit planes of LENA require more than 1 bit/pixel; i.e., the Q-coder results in a data expansion for these planes. This is due to the inherent inefficiency of the Q-coder in encoding a stationary source as discussed in Section 3.5.1. As a result, one might choose to transmit the last two or three bit planes unencoded. In many cases, this strategy results in a smaller bit rate and a simpler implementation.

The primary motivation for using the Gray code is to create decorrelated bit planes that can be encoded independently. However, if information contained in the previously encoded planes can be used in the encoding of the current plane, there is usually little to be gained by using the Gray code representation. One efficient method of incorporating other bit plane information is to extend the context pixel assignment to include pixels from both the current and previous planes. For example, referring to Fig. 6.4, the 7-pixel context can be modified by deleting those pixels in the current bit plane labeled B, C, and G from the context, and instead using the pixels labeled x, A, and E from the previous (more significant) bit plane. Columns 6 and 7 of Table 6.1 summarize the results of applying this 3-D, 7-pixel context configuration to the encoding of the bit planes. As expected, the binary and the Gray code results are almost the same. Furthermore, although the total number of contexts is the same as in the 7-pixel, 2-D configuration, the total bit rates are slightly lower. This is because the 3-D context is a better model of the source and more accurately predicts the current pixel value.

Chapter 7

Lossless Predictive Coding

For typical images, the values of adjacent pixels are highly correlated; that is, a great deal of information about a pixel value can be obtained by inspecting its neighboring pixel values. This property is exploited in predictive coding techniques where an attempt is made to predict the value of a given pixel based on the values of the surrounding pixels. We first describe a general, but impractical, predictive coding scheme and then discuss modifications that yield a practical scheme.

Consider an image modeled as an mth-order Markov source, where each pixel is represented by k bits and can thus take any one of $K(= 2^k)$ possible values. In this model, the value of a given pixel x_m depends only on the values of the m previous pixels, $x_0, x_1, \cdots, x_{m-1}$. The number of possible combinations of the m previous pixel values is K^m, and each combination defines a state of the Markov source. For each state, there is an associated set of K conditional probabilities for the value of the pixel x_m, i.e., $p(x_m|x_{m-1}, \cdots, x_0)$, for $x_m = 0, \cdots, K - 1$. If these conditional probabilities, along with the stationary state probabilities, are known, the entropy of the mth-order Markov source can be calculated according to Eq. (2.5).

In theory, a lossless predictive coding scheme is capable of encoding an image at a bit rate close to this entropy by employing the following strategy. Given the m previous pixel values, the state of the Markov source is defined and the conditional probabilities for the current pixel value $p(x_m|x_{m-1}, \cdots, x_0)$ for $x_m = 0, \cdots, K - 1$ are known. The numbers 0 through $K - 1$ form a set of K predictions (estimates) for the value of x_m given the current state. The prediction that matches the actual value x_m is identified and encoded using a variable-length code optimized for the set of conditional probabilities within that state. Since the decoder also has access to the m previous pixels, it can track the state of the Markov source and hence the corresponding codebook. This allows the decoder to decode the encoded information and identify the actual pixel value x_m.

Unfortunately, the above scheme is impractical in the sense that it requires knowledge of the conditional probabilities within each state and the computation of K^m different codebooks (one for each state), each of which contains K entries. Even for moderate values of K and m, gathering the conditional probabilities and determining (and storing) the codebooks is a formidable task. To provide a practical implementation of the general lossless predictive coding approach, the above strategy can be modified in two ways to reduce the implementation complexity. This modified predictive coding scheme is called lossless *differential pulse code modulation* (DPCM).

- Instead of considering all of the possible estimates for x_m within each state, only the most probable estimate is stored. This requires a look-up table with K^m entries. For each state, the look-up table provides the value $\hat{x}_m$ that maximizes $p(x_m|x_{m-1}, \cdots, x_0)$. The difference between the actual pixel value, x_m, and this most likely prediction, $\hat{x}_m$, is formed and is termed the *differential* or the *error* signal, e_m, i.e.,

$$e_m = x_m - \hat{x}_m. \tag{7.1}$$

  The value of e_m is usually entropy encoded using a single codebook based on the histogram of the differential signal. In this way, there is no need for a separate codebook for each state. The codebook for the differential signal can be computed based on the particular image being encoded (a local codebook) or on a set of images (a global codebook). Note that the technique just described still requires knowledge of the conditional probabilities (since the most likely estimate for each state must be found) and also requires the storage of a potentially large look-up table of size K^m.

- To overcome these difficulties, the prediction can be formed as a linear combination of the m previous pixel values. In this way, no look-up table is required for the most probable estimate and no knowledge of the conditional probabilities is needed. In general, linear prediction is suboptimal compared to the nonlinear prediction that maximizes the conditional probability, but in most cases, this small loss in performance is more than compensated for by the significant reduction in complexity and storage.

In the following sections, we first examine the structure of the linear predictor in more detail and then discuss methods of encoding the differential image.

7.1 DPCM Predictor

Figure 7.1 illustrates the configuration of the previous pixels, x_i, $i = 0, 1, \cdots$, $m - 1$, (denoted in the figure as A, B, C, etc.) that are employed in forming

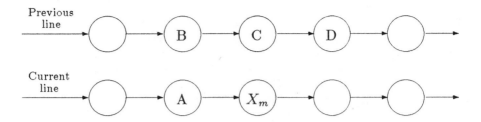

Figure 7.1: DPCM predictor configuration.

the prediction. The number of pixels used in the predictor, m, is called the *order* of the predictor and has a direct bearing on the predictor performance. Generally, a higher order predictor will outperform one of lower order, but studies performed on television images and radiographs have demonstrated that there is only a marginal gain beyond a third-order predictor [7,20].

The set of predictor coefficients may be fixed for all images (global prediction), or may vary from image to image (local prediction), or may even vary within an image to accommodate the local changes in image statistics (adaptive prediction). If an image is characterized as a stationary random field, a set of local predictor coefficients can be derived for each image that minimizes the mean-squared prediction error. However, finding this optimum set of coefficients is computationally intensive as it requires the computation of the image autocorrelation values. Furthermore, images rarely obey the stationary assumption, and as a result, the gain achieved by local prediction is usually small (typically a few percent better compression over global prediction). For the results presented in this section, we use a third-order global predictor of the form

$$\hat{x}_m = 0.75A - 0.50B + 0.75C. \tag{7.2}$$

In Chapter 9: Lossy Predictive Coding, we consider the problem of predictor optimization in more detail.

7.2   Huffman Encoding of Differential Images

The differential image typically has a largely reduced variance compared to the original image and is also significantly less correlated. As an example, Fig. 7.2 shows the original image histograms for LENA and BOOTS, and Fig. 7.3 shows the histograms of the differential images obtained using the

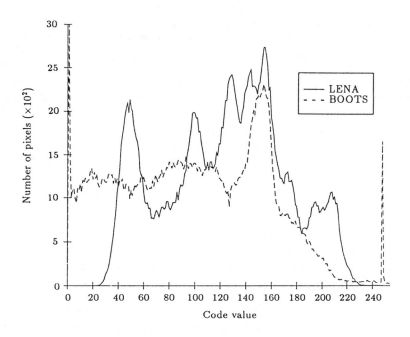

Figure 7.2: Original image histograms.

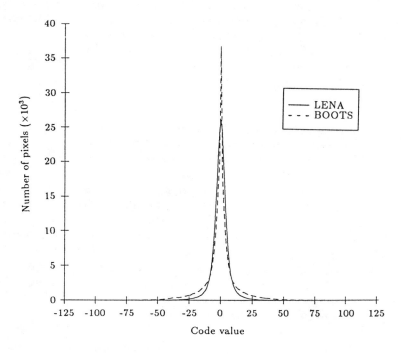

Figure 7.3: Differential image histograms.

predictor described by Eq. (7.2). Since each pixel in the original images is represented by 8 bits, the actual prediction, $\hat{x}_m$, is obtained by rounding off the result of Eq. (7.2) to the nearest integer and clipping to the range [0,255]. The differential signal is then the difference between two 8-bit quantities and can be represented by 9 bits, i.e., values ranging from -255 to 255. The standard deviations of the original images are $\sigma = 47.94$ for LENA and $\sigma = 59.58$ for BOOTS, while the standard deviations of the differential images are only $\sigma_e = 6.94$ and $\sigma_e = 13.37$ for LENA and BOOTS, respectively. The reduction in variance is approximately a factor of 48 for LENA and 20 for BOOTS. As is seen from Fig. 7.3, the histogram of the differential signal is highly peaked around zero and resembles a double-sided exponential distribution of the form

$$p(e) = \frac{1}{\sqrt{2}\sigma_e} \exp(\frac{-\sqrt{2}|x|}{\sigma_e}), \tag{7.3}$$

which is also known as the Laplacian distribution. Studies show that differential signals corresponding to different images roughly have the same shape and only differ in the variance parameter σ_e^2.

The differential image is usually entropy encoded to achieve lossless compression. One approach is to construct a variable-length code, such as a Huffman code, to encode e_m. To encode an image with a local Huffman code that is matched to the statistics of the differential image, a two-pass algorithm is necessary: an initial pass to calculate e_m, determine its histogram, and construct the codebook, and a second pass to encode e_m. One way of eliminating the need for a two-pass algorithm is to construct a Huffman codebook based on an average histogram of e_m. Since the histogram of e_m is fairly stable over a particular image class for a fixed set of predictor coefficients, a global Huffman code usually results only in a small loss in compression efficiency.

The implementation complexity may be further reduced by using a modified Huffman code where all symbols that represent large differences (and are thus less probable) are combined into one symbol. The modified Huffman code can be made even more efficient by noting that the codeword associated with that one symbol can be used as a prefix to the original 8-bit pixel value rather than the 9-bit differential. As an example, Table 7.1 shows the modified local Huffman code corresponding to the LENA image. The table consists of 34 entries: a Huffman code for every difference value that falls in the range $(-16, 16)$ and a prefix code for the values outside that range. This allows the more probable difference values (the values from -16 to $+16$) to be encoded using a small number of bits, while the less probable values (those outside the range -16 to $+16$) can be encoded with 13 bits (5 bits for the prefix and 8 bits for the actual pixel value).

The results of applying lossless DPCM to the two test images are shown in Table 7.2. The first entry in the table is the zeroth-order entropy of the original image and is computed from the original image histogram. It

Difference value	Histogram	Bits	Codeword
-16	667	9	110111000
-15	746	8	00110110
.	.	.	.
.	.	.	.
-7	5421	6	110110
-6	7287	5	01111
-5	9862	5	11010
-4	13271	4	0110
-3	16959	4	1001
-2	21032	4	1110
-1	24755	3	000
0	26040	3	010
1	24387	4	1111
2	20473	4	1100
3	16618	4	1000
4	12650	4	0010
5	9508	5	10110
6	7044	5	00111
7	5109	6	101111
.	.	.	.
.	.	.	.
15	785	8	00110111
16	683	9	110111001
Mag > 16	9337	5	10101

Table 7.1: Local modified Huffman codewords for LENA.

represents the entropy of a DMS with an alphabet of 256 symbols (each symbol representing a certain code value) whose frequencies of occurrence are given by the image histogram. Since the DMS completely ignores the dependence among the pixel values, it is not surprising that the zeroth-order entropy is close to 8 bits. The next entry is the zeroth-order entropy of the differential image, which is computed from the differential image histogram. It is equivalent to the entropy of a DMS with 511 symbols (each representing a difference value in the range -255 to 255) and is a lower bound to the bit rate of any encoding scheme that independently encodes the sequence of differential values. This entropy is significantly less than the zeroth-order entropy of the original image since the pixel correlations have been greatly removed by the prediction process.

Description	LENA image bits/pixel	BOOTS image bits/pixel
Zeroth-order image entropy	7.45	7.49
Zeroth-order differential image entropy	4.56	5.23
Huffman Coding		
Local Huffman code (LHC)	4.60	5.26
Modified LHC $(-64,64)$	4.60	5.27
Modified LHC $(-32,32)$	4.62	5.35
Modified LHC $(-16,16)$	4.69	5.51
Modified LHC $(-8,8)$	4.96	5.76
Global Huffman code (GHC)	4.67	5.34
Modified GHC $(-64,64)$	4.67	5.35
Modified GHC $(-32,32)$	4.67	5.43
Modified GHC $(-16,16)$	4.72	5.61
Modified GHC $(-8,8)$	5.09	5.81
Arithmetic Coding		
Context-based differential entropy (45 contexts)	4.45	4.94
IBM Q-coder bit rate	4.60	4.98

Table 7.2: Lossless predictive coding bit rates.

Next are listed the bit rates for various Huffman codes. The bit rate of the local Huffman code is typically very close to the entropy of the differential signal. In fact, for the two test images, this difference is less than 1%. The global Huffman code is based on the average histogram of 10 images and includes the two test images. As is seen from Table 7.2, the performance difference between the full size local and global Huffman codes is small (on the order of a few percent). Furthermore, the performance of the modified Huffman code (local or global) when designed around the range $(-64, 64)$ is virtually indistinguishable from its corresponding full-size code. Although the modified Huffman code bit rate gradually increases as the codebook size gets smaller, the loss in efficiency compared to a full-size code in our example is less than 5%, even for the $(-16, 16)$ codebook. This makes the global modified Huffman code a viable technique in applications where maintaining a small size codebook is of primary importance.

7.3   Arithmetic Encoding of Differential Images

Although the differential image is significantly less correlated than the original image, it is still slightly correlated. This is because the low-order, linear predictor typically used in DPCM is suboptimal. The Huffman coding procedure described in the previous section does not take advantage of this remaining correlation since it encodes each differential value independent of its neighboring values. If an arithmetic coder is employed that can encode the differential image using contexts based on a pixel's neighboring values, the resultant bit rate can potentially be smaller than the zeroth-order entropy of the differential image.

As noted previously, most practical implementations of arithmetic coding, such as the Q-coder, work only with binary data. Since e_m is represented by a $k + 1$ bit word, direct application of the Q-coder is not possible. Consequently, the use of a binary decision tree has been suggested, whereby the quantity to be encoded is determined by a set of binary decisions and each decision is then encoded by the Q-coder using an appropriate context [21]. A typical decision tree that may be used to encode the differential image is shown in Fig. 7.4. The first level of the tree determines if the differential value is zero. If the value is nonzero, the next decision determines if it is positive or negative. Subsequent decisions determine if the magnitude of e_m is $1, 2, \cdots$, etc. In this fashion, any value in the range $(-255, 255)$ can be determined after a maximum of 256 decisions, although the average number of decisions needed to identify e_m is considerably smaller.[1]

If we encode the binary decisions for a given pixel without considering the neighboring pixel values, the resulting bit rate is lower bounded by the zeroth-order entropy of the differential image. The overall bit rate to encode the decision tree can be found by weighting the entropy of each binary decision by the probability of reaching that decision and then summing over all decisions. For example, referring to Table 7.1, the answer to the first binary question ($e_m = 0$?) for the LENA image is true for 25,931 differential image pixels out of a total of 261,121 pixels. Using the normalized counts as probabilities, we find that the probability of having to encode a "yes" for this decision is about 0.099 and the probability for a "no" is 0.901. The resulting entropy is 0.466 bit/pixel for this decision. This entropy should be weighted by the probability of executing this decision, which is 1.0. The entropy of the next decision ($+$ or $-$) is approximately 1 bit/pixel, since almost half of the nonzero values are positive. The probability of executing this decision is 0.901 since it is reached only if the answer to the first question is "no". Weighting the 1 bit/pixel entropy of this decision by the 0.901 probability of executing it and adding the result to 0.466 bit/pixel from the

---

[1]The sequence in which the binary tree is formed does not significantly affect the final bit rate of the Q-coder, but the Q-coder throughput is directly proportional to the average number of decisions required to identify e_m. As a result, it is desirable to construct a decision tree that minimizes the average number of decisions.

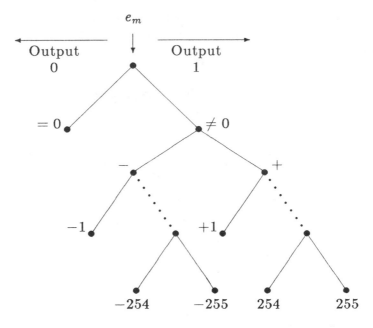

Figure 7.4: Binary decision tree for differential images.

first decision, we get 1.367 bits/pixel. This constitutes the contribution of the first two binary decisions to the overall entropy of the binary decision tree. Proceeding in this manner, the final sum is 4.56 bits/pixel, the same as the zeroth-order entropy of the differential image.

To achieve this bit rate with an adaptive binary arithmetic coder, each decision must be encoded under a separate context (which we term *primary contexts*) to account for the different probability estimates for each decision. Ordinarily, this results in a large number of primary contexts, e.g., 510 contexts for the 9-bit differential signal. One way of reducing the number of primary contexts without significantly affecting the compression efficiency is to encode some of the less probable binary decisions under the same context (i.e., use the same probability estimate for those decisions). Furthermore, binary decisions with approximately the same outcome probability can also be encoded under the same context. For example, we could use a total of five primary contexts: two contexts to encode the first two decisions ($e_m = 0$?, $e_m +$ or$-$?), two contexts to encode a differential value of -1, or $+1$, and finally one more context to encode all the remaining 506 binary decisions. The differential image entropy resulting from the use of only these five primary contexts is 4.59 bits/pixel for LENA and 5.30 bits/pixel for BOOTS, as compared to 4.56 bits/pixel and 5.23 bits/pixel, respectively, if all 510 contexts are used. We see that the entropy increase due to the merging of the contexts is insignificant.

In order to achieve a bit rate lower than the zeroth-order entropy, some or all of the binary decisions must have their outcome probabilities conditioned based on information from the neighboring pixels. As a result, each primary context may further be subdivided into a set of *neighboring contexts* based on the neighboring values. The goal of the conditioning is to deviate the outcome probabilities for a given decision from its average value prior to conditioning, with the result that the decision entropy (averaged over all the conditioning states) is reduced. The challenge is to construct a small, but effective, set of neighboring contexts. It is important to realize that it is not necessary to subdivide all of the primary contexts (as it may result in a large total number of contexts); the conditioning should be performed only where it is most effective.

The neighboring contexts can be defined in a variety of ways. In our example, we consider a scheme that uses a small number of neighboring contexts based on the value of the differential image corresponding to the neighboring pixels A and C. For each neighboring differential image value e_m, three possibilities exist: $(e_m < -7)$, $(-6 \leq e_m \leq 6)$, and $(e_m > 7)$. This creates nine combinations for the possible neighboring differential image values. By conditioning each of the five previously defined primary contexts on these nine neighboring contexts, we get a total of 45 contexts. The entropy of the differential image based on these contexts can be found in Table 7.2, where it has been referred to as the context-based differential entropy. Since this entropy is found by incorporating more information than just the current pixel value, it represents a higher order entropy than the zeroth-order entropy. For example, for the BOOTS image, this context-based entropy is 4.94 bits/pixel, as compared to its zeroth-order entropy of 5.23 bits/pixel. The actual bit rates resulting from the encoding of these contexts by the Q-coder are also given in Table 7.2. As expected, the bit rates are slightly higher than the corresponding entropy values.

Chapter 8

Lossy Plus Lossless Residual Encoding

In most image transmission applications, the requirement of a short transmission time (and correspondingly low bit rate) often precludes the use of a numerically lossless compression algorithm at the outset. However, in certain applications, it may be necessary to send a lossless version of the image at some later stage of the transmission. Such an application might exist in the medical field, where two physicians are discussing a possible patient referral from remote locations. One of the physicians may wish to transmit a digital radiograph over the phone line, and in the interest of a short transmission time, a lossy (but high quality) version of the image is sent. If the referral is accepted, the remaining difference (residual) image required to perfectly reconstruct the original image could be sent, perhaps at the conclusion of the telephone conversation. In general, a lossy plus lossless residual encoding scheme consists of the following steps:

- Generate a low bit rate image through the use of an efficient lossy compression scheme.

- Form a residual by computing the difference between the lossy reconstruction and the original image.

- Encode the residual using an appropriate lossless technique.

A lossy plus residual scheme can be considered a type of predictive coding where the lossy image constitutes a nonlinear, noncausal prediction. The prediction in this case is not based on previously transmitted information as it is in DPCM and must be explicitly transmitted as "overhead." The choice of a particular lossy scheme for this method determines how much information is to be transmitted for the prediction and how much remains in the residual. Any lossy scheme can be used, but obviously some techniques will yield better predictions and/or require less information to form the prediction. We also note that the lossy plus lossless residual approach can be viewed as a simple two-stage progressive transmission technique. This general concept of a prediction/residual encoding approach will appear again in Chapter 12: Vector Quantization and Chapter 14: Hierarchical Coding under Lossy Compression Techniques.

The performance of a lossy plus residual technique using an adaptive discrete cosine transform (DCT) scheme [22] to perform the lossy compression and Huffman and arithmetic coding for the residual has been studied [7]. Variations in the zeroth-order entropy of the residual as a function of the bit rate of the lossy DCT scheme have also been examined [23]. In our study, we selected the JPEG DCT algorithm [24] for the lossy scheme. This algorithm has been proposed as the world standard for the compression of still, continuous-tone images. For more details, the reader is referred to Section 10.5 under Lossy Compression Techniques. Instead of actually encoding the residual, its zeroth-order entropy was computed based on its histogram. These results are summarized in Table 8.1. As expected, increasing the bit rate of the lossy image reduces the entropy of the lossless residual. The total bit rate required to achieve lossless compression varies slightly across the range of DCT bit rates, with a minimum somewhere between 0.75 to 1.00 bit/pixel. A similar observation was made in [23]. In a practical application, the trade-off between the lossy and lossless component bit rates is dictated by where the data overhead can be tolerated.

LENA		
Lossy DCT bits/pixel	**Lossless residual entropy**	**Total bits/pixel**
0.25	4.75	5.00
0.50	4.19	4.69
0.75	3.91	4.66
1.00	3.71	4.71
1.50	3.41	4.91
BOOTS		
Lossy DCT bits/pixel	**Lossless residual entropy**	**Total bits/pixel**
0.25	5.73	5.98
0.50	5.19	5.69
0.75	4.89	5.64
1.00	4.65	5.65
1.50	4.24	5.74

Table 8.1: Lossy plus lossless residual bit rates.

References

[1] A. N. Netravali, ed., Special Issue on Digital Encoding of Graphics, Proc. IEEE, 68(7), (1980).

[2] R. B. Arps, "Binary Image Compression," in W. K. Pratt, ed., *Image Transmission Techniques, Advances in Electronics and Electron Physics,* Supplement 12, Academic Press, Orlando, FL (1979).

[3] H. Tanaka and A. Leon-Garcia, "Efficient run-length encodings," IEEE Trans. Info. Theory, IT-28(6), 880-890 (1982).

[4] M. Rhodes, J. F. Quinn, and J. Silvester, "Locally optimal run-length compression applied to CT images," IEEE Trans. Med. Imag., MI-4(2), 84-90 (1985).

[5] H. Gharavi, "Conditional run-length and variable-length coding of digital pictures," IEEE Trans. Commun., COM-35(6), 671-677 (1987).

[6] K. Takahashi and M. Ohta, "Data compression coding of gray-scale images using bit planes," in *Proc. ICC,* 2.3.1, 34-41 (1985).

[7] S. E. Elnahas, "Data compression with applications to digital radiology," D.Sc. dissertation, Washington Univ., St. Louis, MO (1984).

[8] T. V. Ramabadran and K. Chen, "Efficient compression of medical images through arithmetic coding," in *Proc. SPIE Medical Imaging IV,* 1234, 761-776 (1990).

[9] N. Garcia, C. Munoz, and A. Sanz, "Universal compression lossless code statistically built ," in *Proc. ICASSP,* 48.5.1-48.5.4 (1984).

[10] N. Garcia, C. Munoz, and A. Sanz, "Image compression based on hierarchical encoding," in *Proc. SPIE Symposium on Image Coding,* 594, 150-157 (1985).

[11] S. B. Lo and H. K. Huang, "Error-free and irreversible radiographic image compression," in *Proc. SPIE Picture Archiving and Communication Systems (PACS III),* 536, 170-177 (1985).

[12] M. Nakajima and T. Agui, "Color image coding for pre-press images - reversible coding methods," Bull. Jpn. Soc. Print. Sci. Technol. (in Japanese), 25(1), 2-12 (1987).

[13] C. G. Boncelet, J. R. Cobbs, and A. R. Moser, "Error free compression of medical x-ray images," in *Proc. SPIE Visual Communications and Image Processing '88*, 1001, 269-276 (1988).

[14] P. Roos, M. A. Viergever, M. C. A. van Dijke, and J. H. Peters, "Reversible intraframe compression of medical images," IEEE Trans. Med. Imag., 7(4), 328-336 (1988).

[15] W. B. Pennebaker, J. L. Mitchell, G. G. Langdon, Jr., and R. B. Arps, "An overview of the basic principles of the Q-coder adaptive binary arithmetic coder," IBM J. Res. Dev., 32(6), 717-726 (1988).

[16] R. W. Hamming, *Coding and Information Theory*, 2nd Edition, Prentice-Hall, Englewood Cliffs, NJ, 97-99 (1986).

[17] M. Kunt and O. Johnsen, "Block coding of graphics: a tutorial review," Proc. IEEE, 68(11), 770-786 (1980).

[18] T. S. Huang, "Coding of two-tone images," IEEE Trans. Commun., COM-25(11), 1405-1424 (1977).

[19] G. G. Langdon, Jr. and J. Rissanen, "Compression of black-white images with arithmetic coding," IEEE Trans. Commun., COM-29(6), 858-867 (1981).

[20] A. Habibi, "Comparison of nth-order DPCM encoder with linear transformations and block quantization techniques," IEEE Trans. Commun., COM-19(6), 948-956 (1971).

[21] J. L. Mitchell, "Adaptive binary arithmetic coding for still picture compression," in *Proc. IEEE Picture Coding Symposium*, 9.5.1-9.5.2 (1988).

[22] W. H. Chen and C. H. Smith, "Adaptive coding of monochrome and color images," IEEE Trans. Commun., COM-25(11), 1285-1292 (1977).

[23] J. R. Cox, S. M. Moore, G. J. Blaine, J. B. Zimmerman, and G. K. Wallace, "Optimization of trade-offs in error-free image transmission," in *Proc. SPIE Medical Imaging III*, 1091, 19-30 (1989).

[24] W. Pennebaker, "JPEG Technical Specification, Revision 8," Working Document No. JTC1/SC2/WG10/JPEG-8-R8 (Aug. 1990).

Part IV

Lossy Compression
Techniques

Introduction

In lossy compression schemes, degradations are allowed in the reconstructed image in exchange for a reduced bit rate as compared to lossless schemes. These degradations may or may not be visually apparent, and greater compression can be achieved by allowing more degradation. The general framework for a lossy scheme is shown in Fig. I.1. It includes three components: image decomposition or transformation, quantization, and symbol encoding. The relative importance of each component varies from one lossy technique to another, and not all components are necessarily included in a particular technique. As a general rule, the more sophisticated a scheme is, the better the quality that can be achieved for a given bit rate.

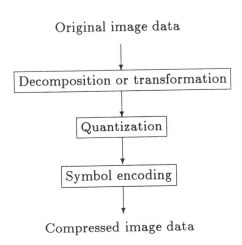

Figure I.1: Lossy compression framework.

The image decomposition or transformation is performed to reduce the dynamic range of the signal, to eliminate redundant information, or, in general, to provide a representation that can be coded more efficiently. This stage is also done in lossless techniques and is generally a reversible operation. For example, in lossless DPCM, a reversible operation is performed on the original image to create the differential image. Although both representations correspond to the same image (and in that respect carry the same amount of information), the zeroth-order entropy of the differential image is significantly lower than that of the original image, and as a result it is more amenable to efficient encoding. The primary difference between lossy and lossless schemes is the inclusion of the next stage, namely, quantization, in lossy techniques. By quantizing the data, the number of possible output symbols is reduced. The type and degree of quantization has a large impact on the bit rate and quality of a lossy scheme. It is also desirable to perform the quantization in such a way that the resulting output sequence can be subsequently encoded efficiently. The symbol encoding process might include techniques such as Huffman coding or arithmetic coding as a means of achieving rates close to the entropy of the quantized symbol source.

In general, any of the components of a lossy scheme may be implemented in an *adaptive* or *nonadaptive* mode. A compression scheme is adaptive if the structure of a component or its parameters changes locally within an image to take advantage of variations in local statistics. Adaptivity offers the potential for improved performance in exchange for an increase in complexity. The adaptivity can be achieved either in a causal or a noncausal fashion.

In systems with *causal adaptivity*, the coder parameters are based only on the previously reconstructed pixel values, and any process leading to a decision at the encoder is duplicated at the decoder. These systems have the advantage of requiring no overhead information. Unfortunately, there are two disadvantages associated with such systems. First, the encoder may fail to adapt to abrupt changes in input statistics that cannot be inferred from previously reconstructed values. Second, causal adaptivity usually increases the complexity of the encoder and the decoder by the same amount since the decoder must duplicate the decision-making process of the encoder.

In systems with *noncausal adaptivity*, the coder parameters are based on previous pixel values (actual or reconstructed) as well as future input values. Since the latter are not available at the decoder, the encoder must send additional bits to the decoder to inform it of any adaptations. Although this results in a higher bit rate, it also increases the overall system performance. Moreover, the increase in decoder complexity due to adaptation is minimal since the decoder does not need to repeat the adaptation selection process of the encoder.

In the following chapters, we discuss a number of different approaches to lossy compression as well as the factors involved in choosing a compression algorithm. The approaches we describe encompass the most popular and widely used techniques, namely, predictive coding, transform coding, block truncation coding (BTC), vector quantization (VQ), and subband coding (SBC). There is also a chapter on hierarchical coding, which is really more of a mode of operation than a specific method. Within each general category, we describe specific implementations and provide results illustrating the performance of these implementations. Each implementation provides relatively high performance within its category (although not necessarily the highest) and was chosen as being a good *representative* of the complexity and performance of that class.

In evaluating the reconstructed image quality provided by each implementation, we make use of root-mean-squared error (RMSE) and peak signal-to-(reconstruction) noise (PSNR) as error metrics. Denoting the original $N \times N$ image by f and the compressed-decompressed image by $\hat{f}$, RMSE is given by

$$\text{RMSE} = \sqrt{\frac{1}{N^2} \sum_{i=1}^{N} \sum_{j=1}^{N} \left[f(i,j) - \hat{f}(i,j) \right]^2}, \tag{I.1}$$

and represents the standard deviation of the error image. The related measure of PSNR (in dB) is computed using

$$\text{PSNR} = 20 \log_{10} \left(\frac{255}{\text{RMSE}} \right) \tag{I.2}$$

for an 8-bit (0-255) image. In the discussions of the various algorithms, we also make use of mean-squared error (MSE), which is defined to be the square of RMSE.

It is important to note that a lower RMSE (or equivalently, a higher PSNR) does not necessarily imply a higher subjective reconstructed image quality; these error metrics do not always correlate well with perceived image quality (although they do provide some measure of relative quality). For this reason, actual reconstructed images are included for each implementation. Error images, representing the difference between the original and reconstructed images, are also shown. The error image, g, is generated using

$$g(i,j) = 2 \left[f(i,j) - \hat{f}(i,j) \right] + 128, \tag{I.3}$$

where the factor of 2 is included to make any errors more visible, and the offset of 128 makes all of the error values positive (for an 8-bit original) so they can be printed on an output device. The error image for a perfectly reconstructed image is a uniform gray field with a code value of 128.

Chapter 9

Lossy Predictive Coding

In a general predictive coding scheme, the correlation between the neighboring pixel values is used to form a prediction for each pixel. By far, the most common approach to predictive coding is *differential pulse code modulation* (DPCM). In DPCM, the prediction is subtracted from the actual pixel value to form a differential image that is much less correlated than the original image data. The differential image is then quantized and encoded. The quantization process determines the resulting bit rate and image quality. We now discuss the components of a lossy DPCM scheme in more detail.

9.1   Differential Pulse Code Modulation (DPCM)

In a lossy DPCM scheme, m pixels within a causal neighborhood of the current pixel are used to make a linear prediction (estimate) of the pixel's value. More specifically, referring to the raster scan configuration in Fig. 7.1, the m pixels prior to the current pixel x_m (shown in the figure as A, B, C, etc.) are used to form a linear prediction denoted by $\hat{x}_m$, where

$$\hat{x}_m = \sum_{i=0}^{m-1} \alpha_i\, x_i, \qquad (9.1)$$

and the α_i's are the predictor coefficients (weighting factors). To reduce the system complexity, the prediction is usually rounded to the nearest integer, although it may be preserved in floating point representation. It is also necessary to clip the prediction to the range $[0, 2^n - 1]$ for an n-bit image. The differential (error) image, e_m, is constructed as the difference between the prediction and the actual value; i.e.,

$$e_m = x_m - \hat{x}_m. \qquad (9.2)$$

As discussed in Chapter 7: Lossless Predictive Coding, the differential image typically has a greatly reduced variance compared to the original image, is significantly less correlated, and has a stable histogram well approximated by a Laplacian (double-sided exponential) distribution [1], given by Eq. (7.3). The difference between lossy and lossless DPCM lies in the handling of the differential image. In order to lower the bit rate, the differential image in lossy DPCM is quantized prior to encoding and transmission. A block diagram for a basic DPCM transmitter and receiver system is shown in Fig. 9.1, where e_m^* represents the quantized differental image.

It is important to realize that in forming a prediction, the receiver only has access to the reconstructed pixel values. Since the quantization of the differential image introduces error, the reconstructed values typically differ from the original values. To assure that identical predictions are formed at both the receiver and the transmitter, the transmitter also bases its predictions on the reconstructed values. This is accomplished by containing the quantizer within the prediction loop as shown in the transmitter diagram of Fig. 9.1. In essence, each DPCM transmitter includes the receiver within its structure.

Transmitter

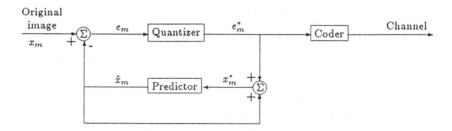

Receiver

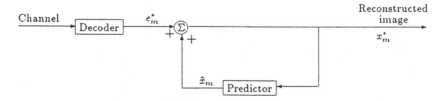

Figure 9.1: DPCM block diagram.

The design of a DPCM system consists of optimizing the predictor and the quantizer components. Because the inclusion of the quantizer in the prediction loop results in a complex dependency between the prediction error and the quantization error, a joint optimization should ideally be performed. However, to avoid the complexity of modeling such interactions, the two components are usually optimized separately. It has been shown that under the mean-squared error optimization criterion, independent optimizations of the predictor and the quantizer are good approximations to the jointly optimal solution [2].

9.1.1 Predictor optimization

The set of predictor coefficients may be fixed for all images (global prediction), or may vary from image to image (local prediction), or may even vary within an image (adaptive prediction). If only pixels from the current scan line are used in forming the prediction, the predictor is referred to as one-dimensional (1-D). If pixels from the previous lines are included, the predictor is two-dimensional (2-D). Quantitatively, 2-D prediction results in SNR improvements of around 3 dB as compared to 1-D prediction, but the subjective quality improvement is even more substantial than this number would suggest. This is mainly due to the elimination of the jaggedness around nonhorizontal edges. The disadvantage of 2-D prediction is that it requires the buffering of the previous line. The number of pixels employed in the prediction is called the *order* of the predictor. In general, a higher order predictor outperforms a lower order one, but studies performed on television images [1] and radiographs [3] have demonstrated that there is only a marginal gain beyond a third-order predictor.

We now address the problem of finding the optimum local (single image) predictor coefficients. A widely used criterion is the minimization of the mean-squared prediction error. Under this criterion, the best linear estimate of x_m is the value $\hat{x}_m$ that minimizes the expected value of the squared prediction error; i.e., it minimizes

$$\sigma_e^2 = E\left\{ \left(x_m - \sum_{i=0}^{m-1} \alpha_i\, x_i \right)^2 \right\}. \tag{9.3}$$

This is realized by making the prediction error orthogonal to all available data, and the m optimal coefficients can thus be found by solving the following set of linear equations [2]:

$$E\left\{ \left(x_m - \sum_{i=0}^{m-1} \alpha_i\, x_i \right) x_i \right\} = 0, \qquad i = 0, 1, \cdots, m-1. \tag{9.4}$$

Expanding this set of equations results in terms involving the image autocorrelation values. Assuming that the image is a 2-D stationary random field, the autocorrelation value $R_{k,l}$ is defined as

$$R_{k,l} = E\{ x(i,j)\, x(i-k, j-l) \},\tag{9.5}$$

where $x(i,j)$ is the pixel value at location (i,j). The need to compute autocorrelation values for each image makes local prediction impractical for many real time applications. Furthermore, the performance gain achieved by a local predictor over a global predictor (one that is fixed for all images) is typically only a few percent. Thus, global prediction is a more attractive choice for most applications.

The selection of a robust set of global predictor coefficients for typical imagery can be approached in a number of ways. One method is to assume a simple image model and then solve the corresponding set of equations given in (9.4). A Markov model with a separable autocorrelation function has been widely used for typical imagery. The autocorrelation function for this model is given by [4,5]

$$R_{k,l} = \bar{x}^2 + \sigma^2 \rho_v^{|k|} \rho_h^{|l|},\tag{9.6}$$

where $\bar{x}$ and σ^2 are the mean and the variance of the image, k and l denote the vertical and horizontal displacements, and ρ_v and ρ_h denote vertical and horizontal correlation coefficients, respectively. For most imagery, ρ_h and ρ_v are typically greater than 0.9. As an example, consider a fourth-order predictor with predictor coefficients α_A, α_B, α_C, and α_D, corresponding to the neighboring pixels A, B, C, and D in Fig. 7.1. Also assume that the image mean has been subtracted from every pixel value, so that $\bar{x} = 0$. Solving the set of equations in (9.4) for this model yields [5]

$$\alpha_A = \rho_h, \quad \alpha_B = -\rho_h \rho_v, \quad \alpha_C = \rho_v, \quad \alpha_D = 0,\tag{9.7}$$

and the resulting predictor is

$$\hat{x}_m = \rho_h A - \rho_h \rho_v B + \rho_v C.\tag{9.8}$$

It is interesting to note that this optimal fourth-order predictor has only three nonzero coefficients rather than four. This is because pixel D contributes no additional information over that already provided by pixels A through C for the particular image model given in Eq. (9.6).

In computing the optimal predictor, the image mean is assumed to be zero. In general, the mean value of the image is not known *a priori*, and its computation results in a two-pass algorithm that is obviously undesirable in a practical implementation. The problem with encoding a nonzero mean image is that the prediction estimate becomes biased. To see this, consider the expected value of the prediction error, i.e., the expected value of the differential image:

$$E\{e_m\} = E\left\{ x_m - \sum_{i=0}^{m-1} \alpha_i\, x_i \right\}$$

$$= E\{x_m\} - \sum_{i=0}^{m-1} \alpha_i\, E\{x_i\}$$

$$= \bar{x}\left(1 - \sum_{i=0}^{m-1} \alpha_i\right). \tag{9.9}$$

When $\bar{x}$ is not zero, the expected value of the differential image will vary from image to image. The obvious solution is to require that the prediction coefficients sum to one; i.e.,

$$\sum_{i=0}^{m-1} \alpha_i = 1, \tag{9.10}$$

which forces the expected value of the differential image to zero regardless of the image mean value. A potential disadvantage of having the coefficients sum to one is that any channel errors are propagated throughout the remainder of the reconstructed image; that is, the reconstruction filter is unstable [5]. Usually, the sum of the coefficients is made slightly less than one (leaky prediction) to reduce the effects of channel errors. Using Eq. (9.7) as a guide and adjusting the coefficients to approximately satisfy the condition in Eq. (9.10), one can get a robust set of predictor coefficients that provide satisfactory performance for a wide variety of images. The following are some examples of typical predictors:

$$\hat{x} = 0.97A, \qquad \text{1st-order, 1-D predictor,} \tag{9.11}$$
$$\hat{x} = 0.50A + 0.50C, \qquad \text{2nd-order, 2-D predictor,} \tag{9.12}$$
$$\hat{x} = 0.90A - 0.81B + 0.90C, \qquad \text{3rd-order, 2-D predictor,} \tag{9.13}$$
$$\hat{x} = 0.75A - 0.50B + 0.75C, \qquad \text{3rd-order, 2-D predictor,} \tag{9.14}$$
$$\hat{x} = A - B + C, \qquad \text{3rd-order, 2-D predictor.} \tag{9.15}$$

9.1.2 Quantizer optimization

A substantial portion of the compression achieved by a lossy DPCM scheme is due to the quantization of the differential image. Quantizer design may be based on either statistical or visual criteria. Several approaches to designing quantizers based on visual criteria have been suggested [6-9], but a debate continues on the best criterion to use, and justifiably so, considering the complexities of the HVS. In the discussion that follows, we restrict ourselves to the design of quantizers that are optimized on a statistical basis.

A quantizer is essentially a staircase function that maps many input values (or even a continuum) into a smaller, finite number of output levels. Let e be a real scalar random variable with a probability density function $p_e(e)$; e.g., e could represent the differential image and $p_e(e)$ could represent its histogram as in Fig. 7.3. A quantizer maps the variable e into a discrete variable e^* that belongs to a finite set $\{r_i, i = 0, \cdots, N-1\}$ of real numbers referred to as *reconstruction levels*. The range of values of e that map to a particular e^* are defined by a set of points $\{d_i, i = 0, \cdots, N\}$, referred to as *decision levels*. The quantization rule states that if e lies in the interval $(d_i, d_{i+1}]$, it is mapped (quantized) to r_i, which also lies in the same interval. The quantizer design problem is to determine the optimum decision and reconstruction levels for a given $p_e(e)$ and a given optimization criterion.

Depending on whether the quantizer output levels are encoded using variable-length or fixed-length codewords, two different types of quantizers are typically used in a DPCM system. For fixed-length codewords, the DPCM bit rate is proportional to $\log_2 N$, where N is the number of quantizer levels. In this case, it is desirable to design a quantizer that minimizes the quantization error for a given N. If the MSE criterion is used, this approach leads to a quantizer known as the Lloyd-Max quantizer [10,11]. This type of quantizer has nonuniform decision regions. For variable-length codewords, the bit rate is lower bounded by the entropy of the quantizer output (instead of $\log_2 N$), which leads to the approach of minimizing the quantization error subject to an entropy constraint. Since the quantizer output distribution is usually highly skewed, the use of variable-length coding seems appropriate. For a Laplacian density and MSE distortion, the optimum quantizer in this case is uniform [12,13]; i.e., the decision regions all have the same width. For the same MSE distortion, a uniform quantizer has more levels than a Lloyd-Max quantizer, but it also has a lower output entropy. It has been shown that for Laplacian density and a large number of quantizer levels, optimum variable-length coding improves the SNR by about 5.6 dB over fixed-length coding at the same bit rate [14].

It is worthwhile to discuss the Lloyd-Max quantizer in more detail since it finds use in other techniques besides DPCM. Its derivation is based on minimizing the expression

$$D = \sum_{i=0}^{N-1} \int_{d_i}^{d_{i+1}} (e - r_i)^2 \, p_e(e) \, de \qquad (9.16)$$

with respect to $\{d_i, i = 0, 1, \cdots, N\}$ and $\{r_i, i = 0, \cdots, N-1\}$. The solution results in decision levels that are halfway between the neighboring reconstruction levels and reconstruction levels that lie at at the center of the mass of the probability density enclosed by the two adjacent decision levels, i.e., at the mean of the differential image in that interval. Mathematically, the decision and reconstruction levels are solutions to the following set of nonlinear equations:

$$d_i = \frac{r_{i-1} + r_i}{2}, \qquad (9.17)$$

$$r_i = \int_{d_i}^{d_{i+1}} e \, p_e(e) \, de \Big/ \int_{d_i}^{d_{i+1}} p_e(e) \, de. \qquad (9.18)$$

In general, Eqs. (9.17) and (9.18) do not yield closed-form solutions, and they need to be solved by numerical techniques [15]. In certain cases, such as the Laplacian pdf, a closed-form solution exists [16]. When a numerical solution is necessary, the following iterative algorithm can be used [10]. First, an arbitrary initial set of values for $\{d_i\}$ is chosen, and the optimum $\{r_i\}$ for that set are found by using Eq. (9.18). For the calculated $\{r_i\}$, the optimum $\{d_i\}$ are then determined using Eq. (9.17). This process is iterated until the difference between two successive approximations is below a threshold. In most cases, rapid convergence is achieved for a wide range of initial values.

Figure 9.2 shows the optimum Lloyd-Max decision and reconstruction levels for a unit-variance Laplacian density with $N = 8$ (3-bit quantizer). As expected, the quantization is fine near zero where the signal pdf is large, and becomes coarse for large differences. To illustrate typical performance, the 3-bit quantizer (scaled according to the prediction error variance) was applied to the LENA image. The results are summarized in Table 9.1. The first column denotes the index i of the quantizer output. The second column denotes the decision and reconstruction levels for a given quantizer level. Note that the magnitude of the largest reproducible difference value in this system is only 20. Due to the required symmetry, a quantizer with an even number of levels cannot reconstruct a difference of zero. This type of quantizer is referred to as a *mid-riser* quantizer. It is also possible to design a *mid-tread* quantizer that has an odd number of levels and can pass zero. If the levels are fixed-length coded, the mid-tread quantizer is less efficient because of unused codewords. The third column shows the probabilities of occurrence of the quantizer outputs. The entropy of the quantizer output levels is 2.52 bits/pixel while the local Huffman code in the last column of Table 9.1 achieves a bit rate of 2.57 bits/pixel, which is fairly close to the entropy. As noted previously, the use of an optimum uniform quantizer with variable-length coding would allow for a higher quality reconstruction at this same bit rate, or conversely, a lower bit rate for the same quality.

In designing a quantizer for a given application, it is important to understand the types of visual distortion introduced by the quantization process in DPCM, namely, *granular noise*, *slope overload*, and *edge busyness* [17]. These are illustrated in Fig. 9.3. Granular noise is apparent in uniform regions and results from the quantizer output fluctuating randomly between the inner levels as it attempts to track small differential signal magnitudes. The use of small inner levels or a mid-tread quantizer with zero as an output level may help to reduce granular noise. Slope overload noise occurs at high contrast edges when the outer levels of the quantizer are not large enough to respond quickly to large differential signals. A lag of several pixels is required for the quantizer to track the differential signal, resulting in a smoothing of the edge. Edge busyness occurs when a reconstructed edge varies slightly in its position from one scan line to another due to quantizer fluctuations. Unfortunately, attempts to reduce one type of degradation usually enhance other types of noise.

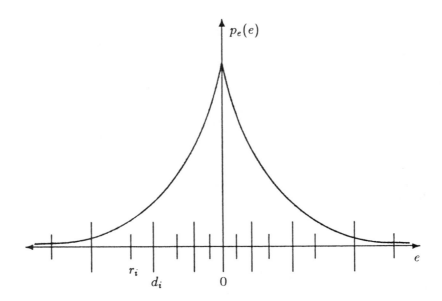

Figure 9.2: 8-level Lloyd-Max quantizer.

i	$(d_i, d_{i+1}) \rightarrow r_i$	Probability	Huffman code
0	$(-255, -16) \rightarrow -20$	0.025	111111
1	$(-16, -8) \rightarrow -11$	0.047	11110
2	$(-8, -4) \rightarrow -6$	0.145	110
3	$(-4, 0) \rightarrow -2$	0.278	00
4	$(0, 4) \rightarrow 2$	0.283	10
5	$(4, 8) \rightarrow 6$	0.151	01
6	$(8, 16) \rightarrow 11$	0.049	1110
7	$(16, 255) \rightarrow 20$	0.022	111110

Table 9.1: 8-level Lloyd-Max quantizer for LENA.

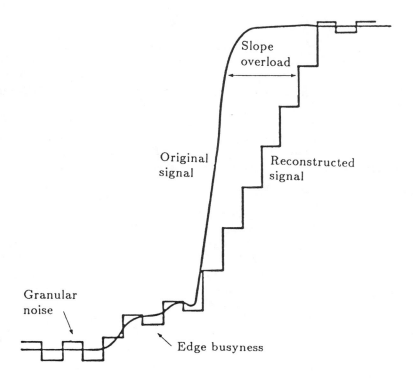

Figure 9.3: Types of DPCM noise.

9.2 Adaptive DPCM

A major limitation of the DPCM system considered so far is that the predictor and the quantizer are both fixed throughout the image. DPCM schemes can be made adaptive in terms of the predictor or the quantizer or both. Adaptive prediction usually reduces the prediction error prior to quantization, and thus, for the same bit rate, the reduced dynamic range of the quantizer input signal results in less quantization error and better reconstructed image quality. On the other hand, adaptive quantization aims at reducing the quantization error directly by varying the decision and reconstruction levels according to the local image statistics. We now review several adaptive DPCM (ADPCM) prediction and quantization schemes to provide more insight into the implementation of the above concepts [18].

9.2.1   Adaptive prediction

Nonadaptive predictors generally perform poorly at edges where abrupt changes in pixel values occur. An adaptive scheme has been proposed to improve the prediction in such regions [19]. The scheme is based on switching among a set of predictors based on the most likely direction of the edge. In particular, the prediction is chosen to be one of the previous pixel values, A, B, C, or D, as in Fig. 7.1. In determining the edge direction, the reconstructed values of the neighboring pixels are used so that the decision is causal. Improved perceived image quality and SNR gains of approximately 4 dB were reported for this method as compared to a third-order fixed predictor.

In another causal technique, the prediction value of a conventional 2-D predictor is multiplied by an adaptive coefficient k to generate a new prediction [20]. The value of the coefficient is based on the previous quantizer reconstruction level. For example, if the previous reconstruction level has been a positive maximum, there is a high probability of a slope overload, and thus k is chosen to be greater than one to accommodate the large positive difference. With this relatively simple adaptive technique, the slope response in DPCM systems using 3 bits/pixel or less can be improved.

9.2.2   Adaptive quantization

In the adaptive prediction technique just described, the prediction was scaled based on the previous reconstruction level. Using the same idea, an adaptive quantizer scheme can also be developed. In this approach, the quantizer levels for a given pixel are found by scaling the levels used for the previous pixel by some factor [21]. This factor depends on the reconstruction level used for the previous pixel, so no overhead information is required. It was reported that proportionately faster step size increases were needed as compared to the step size decreases. It was also found that with increasing number of quantizer levels, the performance improvement of this approach over a fixed quantizer scheme became less pronounced. The scheme is particularly effective with one-bit DPCM, also known as *delta modulation* (DM).

A more sophisticated approach to adaptive quantization is to make use of the visual masking effects in the HVS [9]. It is well known that the luminance sensitivity of the HVS decreases in the picture areas of high-contrast detail. In these areas, large quantization errors can be masked by the HVS. In [8], a procedure was outlined for designing quantizers with the minimum number of output levels, subject to the constraint that the largest magnitude of the quantization error resulting from an arbitrary input is less than the visibility threshold. Using these types of quantizers, adaptivity can be introduced by considering the degree of noise masking possible around the current pixel (based on surrounding image detail) and then switching among a number of quantizers. The detail or activity in a neighborhood around the current pixel can be defined in a number of different ways. For example, the weighted average of several vertical and horizontal gradients can be used. If a noncausal neighborhood is used in determining the activity, overhead information must be transmitted to inform the receiver of the quantizer selection.

In another noncausal method [22], an estimate of the number of bits required to quantize the differential signal is made for each pixel. This estimate is based on the previously reconstructed differential values and can be tracked by the receiver. For each pixel, one bit of overhead information is transmitted denoting the validity of the estimate. For example, a '0' implies that the estimated number of bits was sufficient for encoding the differential image and is followed by the information needed to identify the selected quantizer level. A '1' indicates that more bits are required than estimated and is followed by a '0' for each skipped quantization level until it is terminated by '1' at the desired quantization level. The overhead information, if left uncompressed, adds at least 1 bit/pixel to the overall bit rate of the system. Fortunately, the entropy of the overhead signal is small and can be entropy encoded using adaptive arithmetic coding techniques.

A third scheme using noncausal adaptation is based on the observation that the distribution of the differential signal e_m is generally a function of the neighboring (past and future) pixel values [23,24]. Nonadaptive quantizers assume that e_m has a Laplacian pdf with a variance equal to the global variance of the differential image. However, for a given set of neighboring values, the actual distribution of e_m may substantially differ from that assumption. For example, the variance of e_m in flat regions is much smaller than the global variance, whereas the variance in highly textured areas may be larger than the global value. Also, near contours or high-contrast edges, the distribution may not even be symmetric. As a result, instead of using a single quantizer, the system switches among a set of quantizers designed to accommodate the varying local statistics. In a practical system, to reduce overhead bits and computational complexity, the selection of a given quantizer can be made for a block of the image rather than each individual pixel. The following steps summarize the action of the encoder:

- Partition each scan line into blocks of k pixels.

- Encode the block using each of the m available quantizers.

- Measure the distortion resulting from each quantizer.

- Select the quantizer with minimum distortion.

- Transmit $\log_2 m$ bits of overhead information per k-pixel block to identify the quantizer to the receiver.

- Transmit the encoded signal for the block.

A block diagram of the encoder is shown in Fig. 9.4. It is evident from the above description that there are several parameters which need to be selected in the design and implementation of the switched quantizer scheme, namely, the length of the image block, the number of quantizers, the structure of each individual quantizer, and the distortion measure.

A larger block size implies a smaller overhead penalty, but also reduces the advantages gained from the adaptivity. In [25], a value of $k = 6$ is used, whereas the value of k used in [23] is 16. In our example, we found that $k = 10$ was a good compromise.

In general, choosing the number of quantizers is a trade-off between improving the reconstructed image quality and keeping the overhead bits at an acceptable level. The number of quantizers used in [23] is four. In [25], seven quantizers and a runlength option are used. With a fixed-length code, the value of m is restricted to a power of two, but with entropy coders such as an arithmetic coder, m can have any value. In our example, we used four quantizers and employed fixed-length codes to encode the overhead information.

Ideally, for a given m, it is desirable to design the quantizers so that the overall quantization distortion is minimized. Due to the complexity of this problem, the quantizer design has usually been performed in an *ad hoc* manner. In [23], the quantizers are symmetric and are scaled versions of the Lloyd-Max quantizer for a Laplacian pdf with a variance equal to the global variance of the differential image. In [25], it was argued that nonsymmetric quantizers can encode edges more effectively. This is particularly true for small block sizes. Also, the number of output quantizer levels does not have to be fixed and can be allowed to vary for different quantizers. Varying the number of output quantizer levels generally results in superior image quality, but it also gives rise to a variable output rate, which may not be desirable in certain applications. Furthermore, in such a case, the selection of the optimum quantizer becomes a complicated task as a certain quantizer may result in higher distortion but also a lower bit rate. In our example, we used symmetric quantizers with eight reconstruction levels, which were all scaled versions of the global Lloyd-Max quantizer.

The distortion measure used in selecting the quantizer for each block should ideally be based on visual criteria. Implementing such a measure requires a good knowledge of HVS and is computationally intensive. As a result, simpler distortion measures such as MSE are commonly used. An alternative distortion measure is the sum of the absolute error. This measure has an advantage in hardware implementation as the absolute value operation requires less circuitry than the squaring operation. We have found that both distortion measures work well in practice for this application.

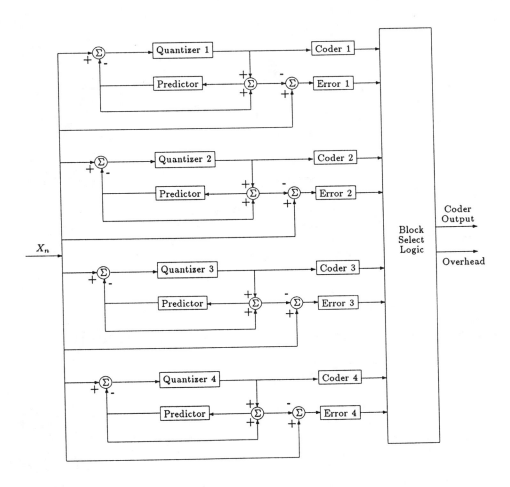

Figure 9.4: Block diagram for adaptive DPCM using switched quantization.

9.3   DPCM Results

Table 9.2 summarizes the results obtained from applying nonadaptive and adaptive (switched quantization) DPCM techniques to the two test images using fixed 1-D and 2-D predictors. The 1-D predictor was $\hat{X} = 0.97A$, and the 2-D predictor was $\hat{X} = 0.75A - 0.50B + 0.75C$. In the nonadaptive DPCM scheme, Lloyd-Max nonuniform quantizers with two, four, or eight output levels (corresponding to a bit rate of 1.00, 2.00, or 3.00 bits/pixel with fixed-length coding) were used to quantize the differential image. These quantizers were optimized for a Laplacian distribution with the same variance as the differential image global variance.

The ADPCM scheme switched among four $(m = 4)$ quantizers over a block length of 10 pixels $(k = 10)$. The overhead information required to inform the receiver of the quantizer choice was thus 2 bits/10 pixels = 0.2 bit/pixel. All quantizers were scaled versions of the same Lloyd-Max nonuniform quantizers used in the nonadaptive case. The scale factors were 0.50, 1.00, 1.75, and 2.50. With the overhead information, the resulting bit rates were 1.20, 2.20, and 3.20 bits/pixel.

Figures 9.5 - 9.7 show reconstructed and error images for LENA using the nonadaptive DPCM with the 2-D predictor at 1.00, 2.00, and 3.00 bits/pixel. Figure 9.8 is a magnified section of LENA (the right eye) to illustrate the performance and artifacts of nonadaptive DPCM at 2.00 bits/pixel in comparison to the original image. Figures 9.9 - 9.11 show reconstructed and error images for the switched quantization ADPCM technique at 1.20, 2.20, and 3.20 bits/pixel.

9.4   Implementation Issues and Complexity of ADPCM Algorithm

In the following discussion on the ADPCM computational complexity, it is assumed that the switched quantizer encoder is implemented as four independent sequential encoder units; i.e., we do not take advantage of the common components in the predictor computations or the parallel nature of the switched quantizer. A parallel implementation of the four quantizers could easily be implemented to effectively reduce the number of computations.

For each encoder unit, the third-order predictor requires 3 multiplications and 2 additions per pixel, and formation of the differential, reconstructed, and distortion signals requires 3 additions per pixel. Each scalar quantizer of rate R ($R = 1$, 2, or 3 bits) requires R comparisons per pixel if a binary tree structure, i.e., successive approximation, is used. Therefore, the four encoder units require a total of

Technique	Bit rate bits/pixel	LENA		BOOTS	
		RMSE (0-255)	SNR (dB)	RMSE (0-255)	SNR (dB)
1-D DPCM	1.00	18.67	22.71	22.79	20.98
1-D DPCM	2.00	9.44	28.63	10.96	27.33
1-D DPCM	3.00	5.11	33.96	5.33	33.60
2-D DPCM	1.00	14.58	27.74	15.91	24.10
2-D DPCM	2.00	6.93	31.32	7.70	30.40
2-D DPCM	3.00	3.71	36.74	4.01	36.07
1-D ADPCM	1.20	10.91	27.37	14.12	25.13
1-D ADPCM	2.20	4.37	35.32	5.97	32.61
1-D ADPCM	3.20	2.16	41.44	3.16	38.14
2-D ADPCM	1.20	7.84	30.24	10.20	27.96
2-D ADPCM	2.20	2.87	38.97	4.75	34.60
2-D ADPCM	3.20	1.37	45.40	2.56	39.97

Table 9.2: DPCM results.

- 12 multiplications,

- 20 additions, and

- $4R$ comparisons

per pixel. We disregard the additional 3 comparisons per 10 pixel block required to choose the minimum distortion quantizer. The decoder requires 3 multiplications and 2 additions per pixel for the predictor and 1 addition to form the reconstructed value.

Therefore, the decoder requires

- 3 multiplications and

- 3 additions

per pixel. The asymmetry between the encoder and decoder is obvious for this algorithm.

Memory requirements are minimal for the ADPCM algorithm. At both the encoder and decoder, permanent memory is required for the predictor coefficients and the quantizer levels, and two line buffers are required to store the previous and current reconstructed lines used in the predictor computations. Four block buffers are also required at the encoder for the switched quantizer selection.

As noted in Section 9.1.1, channel errors are propagated in DPCM owing to the use of previously reconstructed values in the predictor. The errors are typically manifested as 1-D or 2-D streaks (depending on whether the predictor is 1-D or 2-D), and the extent of the streaks depends on the values of the predictor coefficients. The effects of any channel errors can be minimized by sending the actual values of pixels at prescribed locations in order to reinitialize the predictor at both the transmitter and the receiver.

Figure 9.5: DPCM at 1.00 bit/pixel.

Figure 9.6: DPCM at 2.00 bits/pixel.

Figure 9.7: DPCM at 3.00 bits/pixel.

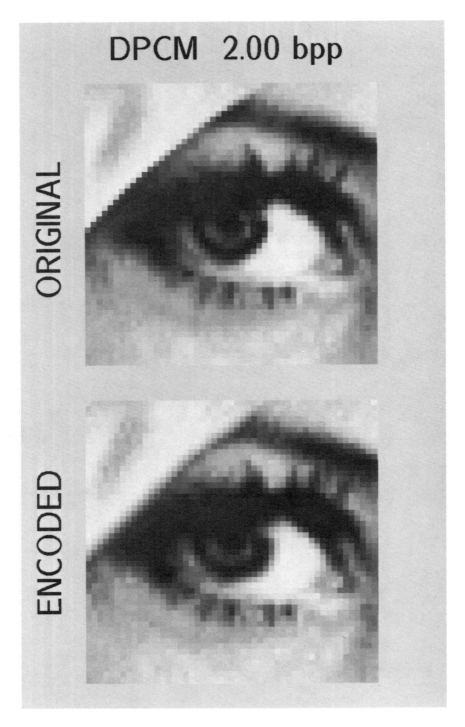

Figure 9.8: DPCM at 2.00 bits/pixel (magnified).

Figure 9.9: ADPCM at 1.20 bits/pixel.

Figure 9.10: ADPCM at 2.20 bits/pixel.

Figure 9.11: ADPCM at 3.20 bits/pixel.

Chapter 10

Transform Coding

A general transform coding scheme involves subdividing an $N \times N$ image into smaller $n \times n$ blocks and performing a *unitary transform* on each subimage. A unitary transform is a reversible linear transform whose kernel describes a set of complete, orthonormal discrete basis functions [26]. The goal of the transform is to decorrelate the original signal, and this decorrelation generally results in the signal energy being redistributed among only a small set of transform coefficients. In this way, many coefficients can be discarded after quantization and prior to encoding. Also, visually lossless compression can often be achieved by incorporating the HVS contrast sensitivity function in the quantization of the coefficients. A block diagram of a basic transform coding scheme is shown in Fig. 10.1.

A transform is referred to as one-dimensional (1-D) if it is performed along a single dimension of the image, i.e., along a line or a column of pixels. A 1-D transform performed on n pixels is termed an *n-point transform*. A transform is two-dimensional (2-D) if it is performed on a 2-D block of pixels. All of the 2-D transforms considered in this chapter are *separable* in that the transform kernel can be decomposed into two 1-D kernels specifying separate horizontal and vertical operations. Thus, a separable transform on an $n \times n$ block of pixels can be performed in two steps. First, a 1-D n-point transform is performed along each row of the block and then another 1-D n-point transform is performed along each column of the resulting output.

There are several ways in which an n-point unitary transform can be interpreted [26]. One approach is to consider it as a rotation of the n-dimensional coordinate axes defined by the image pixels in a block. Another view is that the transform decomposes the original block into a set of n orthogonal basis functions. In the following sections, we elaborate on each of these interpretations.

Transmitter

Receiver

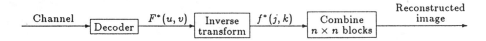

Figure 10.1: Transform coding block diagram.

10.1   Transforms as Coordinate Axes Rotations

Consider a simple 1-D transform that operates on 1×2 pixel blocks, i.e., a 2-point transform. Referring to Fig. 10.2, every two-dimensional vector $\mathbf{X}$ in the $x_1 x_2$-coordinate system represents a pair of adjacent pixel values. The scatter plot in Fig. 10.2 was obtained by plotting all of the pixel pairs in the LENA image. Since adjacent pixels are typically highly correlated, most of the points lie along the 45^0 line defined by $x_1 = x_2$. The variance in the x_j $(j = 1, 2)$ direction is defined as

$$\sigma_{x_j}^2 = \frac{1}{M} \sum_{i=1}^{M} (x_{ji} - \overline{x_j})^2, \qquad (10.1)$$

where M is the total number of blocks in the image, and $\overline{x_j}$ is the mean value of x_j over all blocks. A simple way to achieve compression is to represent one of the components (either x_1 or x_2) in each block by its corresponding mean value $\overline{x_j}$.[1] The MSE introduced in the reconstructed image by this encoding method is equal to $\sigma_{x_j}^2$. Unfortunately, it is evident from Fig. 10.2

---

[1]When a random variable (such as a pixel value) is replaced by a constant, the resulting MSE is minimized if the constant is equal to the mean of the random variable.

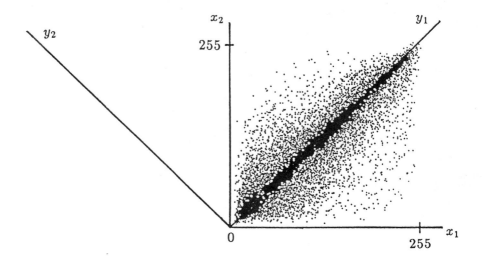

Figure 10.2: Rotation transform example.

that the variance in both the x_1 and x_2 directions is large, and as a result, encoding either x_1 or x_2 by its corresponding mean value will result in large reconstruction errors.

Now consider a unitary transform of the vector $\mathbf{X}$ into the vector $\mathbf{Y} = (y_1, y_2)$ by rotating the $x_1 x_2$-coordinate axes by 45^0; i.e.,

$$\begin{bmatrix} y_1 \\ y_2 \end{bmatrix} = \frac{1}{\sqrt{2}} \begin{bmatrix} 1 & 1 \\ -1 & 1 \end{bmatrix} \begin{bmatrix} x_1 \\ x_2 \end{bmatrix},$$

or equivalently,

$$\mathbf{Y} = \mathbf{AX}, \tag{10.2}$$

where $\mathbf{A}$ is the rotation matrix. Equation (10.2) defines the *forward transform*. An important feature of a unitary transform is that it is distance preserving; i.e., it does not change the Euclidean distance between vectors. This can be used to show that the total variance (energy) of the data is preserved by the rotation; i.e.,

$$\sigma_{x_1}^2 + \sigma_{x_2}^2 = \sigma_{y_1}^2 + \sigma_{y_2}^2. \tag{10.3}$$

As demonstrated by Fig. 10.2, the energy in the original image is more or less equally distributed in both the x_1 and x_2 directions ($\sigma_{x_1}^2 \approx \sigma_{x_2}^2$), but the energy distribution along the y_1 and y_2 axes in the transformed data is highly skewed ($\sigma_{y_1}^2 \gg \sigma_{y_2}^2$). This is an example of the *energy packing* property that is desirable in a transform. If the y_2 component is replaced by its mean value (which is zero) during encoding, the resultant MSE is only $\sigma_{y_2}^2$, which is significantly less than either $\sigma_{x_1}^2$ or $\sigma_{x_2}^2$.

It is important to realize that the transform operation itself does not achieve any compression; it aims at decorrelating the original data and compacting a large fraction of the signal energy into a relatively few transform components. Since the total energy is preserved, many of the transform coefficients will contain very little energy. It is the subsequent quantization of these coefficients and their efficient encoding that results in compression. The level of compression usually depends on the degree of quantization performed; coarser quantization results in higher compression but also introduces more degradation. In general, reconstruction quality can be traded for bit rate through the adjustment of the quantizer.

Since a unitary transform is reversible, the original data can be recovered if no errors are introduced by the encoding process. The rotation transform in the above example can be reversed by performing the *inverse transform*, which is a rotation by -45^0; i.e.,

$$\left[\begin{array}{c} x_1 \\ x_2 \end{array} \right] = \frac{1}{\sqrt{2}} \left[\begin{array}{cc} 1 & -1 \\ 1 & 1 \end{array} \right] \left[\begin{array}{c} y_1 \\ y_2 \end{array} \right],$$

or in matrix notation,

$$\mathbf{X} = \mathbf{BY}, \tag{10.4}$$

where $\mathbf{B} = \mathbf{A}^{-1}$. It is useful to note that for unitary transforms, $\mathbf{A}^{-1} = \mathbf{A}^{\star T}$, where $\star$ denotes the complex conjugate. In a practical encoding scheme, the transform coefficients are quantized, and the inverse transform of the quantized coefficients results in an approximation to the original image. Because of the distance-preserving property of the rotation, the MSE between the original image and the reconstructed image is equal to the MSE introduced by the quantization process in the transform domain.

10.2 Transforms as Basis Function Decompositions

In the previous example, we saw how a simple coordinate system rotation could transform the original vector into an equivalent vector whose properties are more amenable to compression. All of the image transforms considered in this chapter can be viewed as a rotation of the coordinate axes in higher dimensions. The various transforms merely differ in the nature of the rotation.

A different interpretation of transforms can be found by examining Eq. (10.4). We can view the columns of the matrix $\mathbf{B}$ as discrete orthogonal *basis functions* which when weighted by the *transform coefficients* $\mathbf{Y}$ and added together result in the original data $\mathbf{X}$. The basis functions differ for each type of image transform and can be considered as elementary components that can be used to synthesize an image given its corresponding transform coefficients. Similarly, the forward transform given in Eq. (10.2) can be viewed as a decomposition of the original data into a set of transform coefficients for a given set of basis functions.

Since the basis functions for the discrete Fourier transform (DFT) consist of sines and cosines of different frequency, it is natural to also interpret this transform as a *spectral decomposition* of the original image. This interpretation can be extended to other transforms if the concept of frequency is generalized to include functions other than sines and cosines. For example, in the Hadamard transform, rectangular waveforms with increasing number of sign changes (referred to as *sequency*) are used as the basis functions. Each transform coefficient is proportional to the fraction of the energy in the original image that corresponds to that particular spectral function.

10.3   Image Transforms

There are several characteristics that are desirable in a transform when it is used for the purpose of image compression.

- Image decorrelation: The ideal transform completely decorrelates the data in a block; that is, it packs the most amount of energy in the fewest number of coefficients.

- Image-independent basis functions: Owing to the large statistical variations among images, the optimum transform usually depends on the image. Unfortunately, finding the basis functions of such a transform is a computationally intensive task. This is particularly a problem if the image blocks are highly nonstationary, which necessitates the use of more than one set of basis functions to achieve high decorrelation. Also, the overhead required to transmit these sets of basis functions to the decoder can lower the compression efficiency. As a result, it is generally desirable to trade off optimum performance for a transform whose basis functions are image-independent.

- Fast implementation: The number of operations required for a n-point transform is generally on the order of $\mathcal{O}(n^2)$. Some transforms have fast implementations, which reduces the number of operations to $\mathcal{O}(n \log n)$. For a separable $n \times n$ 2-D transform, performing the row and column 1-D transforms in succession reduces the number of operations to $\mathcal{O}(2n^2 \log n)$ instead of $\mathcal{O}(n^4)$.

In the following sections, brief descriptions of widely used transforms for image compression are presented.

10.3.1 Karhunen-Loève transform (KLT)

The KLT is the optimal transform in an energy-packing sense; i.e., if only a limited number of transform coefficients are retained, the KLT coefficients will contain a larger fraction of the total energy as compared to any other transform. Unfortunately, the KLT basis functions are image-dependent and require an estimate of the image covariance function for their computation. Furthermore, a fast KLT algorithm does not exist. These drawbacks severely limit its utility for image compression.

10.3.2 Discrete Fourier transform (DFT)

The DFT is commonly used for spectral analysis and filtering. For an $n \times n$ block of pixels, f, the forward 2-D DFT is defined as [26]

$$F(u,v) = \frac{1}{n} \sum_{j=0}^{n-1} \sum_{k=0}^{n-1} f(j,k) \exp\left\{ -\frac{2\pi i(uj+vk)}{n} \right\}, \qquad (10.5)$$

and the inverse 2-D DFT is defined as

$$f(j,k) = \frac{1}{n} \sum_{u=0}^{n-1} \sum_{v=0}^{n-1} F(u,v) \exp\left\{ \frac{2\pi i(uj+vk)}{n} \right\}, \qquad (10.6)$$

where $i = \sqrt{-1}$. The DFT essentially decomposes the image block into its spectral components, and the indices u and v are called the spatial frequencies of the transform. The 2-D kernel is separable; i.e.,

$$\exp\left\{ \frac{2\pi i(uj+vk)}{n} \right\} = \exp\left\{ \frac{2\pi iuj}{n} \right\} \exp\left\{ \frac{2\pi ivk}{n} \right\},$$

which allows the 2-D transform to be implemented as two 1-D transforms. Extensive study has been done on fast implementations of the DFT (known as fast Fourier transforms, or FFTs), which typically requires $O(n \log_2 n)$ for an n-point transform [27].

In general, the transform coefficients generated by the DFT are complex, (i.e., they consist of real and imaginary components, or magnitude and phase components), and the storage and manipulation of these complex quantities can be a decided disadvantage. There are actually a total of $2n^2$ transform components, but because of the conjugate symmetry property,

$$F(u,v) = F^*(-u+ln, -v+mn), \qquad l,m = 0,1,2,\ldots, \qquad (10.7)$$

almost half of the transform components are redundant and can be computed from other components [26]. Another disadvantage of the DFT is that spurious spectral components are generated due to the implicit periodicity of the image blocks. When encoded at low bit rates, these spurious components can give rise to severe blocking artifacts. This characteristic is discussed in more detail in the following section on the discrete cosine transform.

10.3.3   Discrete cosine transform (DCT)

For image processing applications, the forward 2-D DCT of an $n \times n$ block of pixels is often defined as [28]

$$F(u, v) = \frac{4C(u)C(v)}{n^2} \sum_{j=0}^{n-1} \sum_{k=0}^{n-1} f(j, k) \, \cos\left[\frac{(2j+1)u\pi}{2n}\right] \cos\left[\frac{(2k+1)v\pi}{2n}\right],$$

(10.8)

and the inverse 2-D DCT is defined as

$$f(j, k) = \sum_{u=0}^{n-1} \sum_{v=0}^{n-1} C(u)C(v)F(u, v) \, \cos\left[\frac{(2j+1)u\pi}{2n}\right] \cos\left[\frac{(2k+1)v\pi}{2n}\right],$$

(10.9)

where

$$C(w) = \begin{cases} \frac{1}{\sqrt{2}} & \text{for } w = 0 \\ 1 & \text{for } w = 1, 2, \ldots, n-1. \end{cases}$$

(10.10)

For typical images that exhibit high pixel-to-pixel correlation, the performance of the DCT is virtually indistinguishable from the KLT. In fact, it can be shown that for a first-order Markov source model, as the adjacent pixel correlation coefficient approaches unity, the DCT basis functions become identical to the KLT basis functions of the image data [29]. The DCT basis functions for an 8×8 block are shown in Fig. 10.3. The normalized basis functions have been scaled by 128 and biased by 127 to make them suitable for the 8-bit output device that was used.

Like the DFT, the DCT has a fast implementation with a computational complexity of $\mathcal{O}(n \log n)$ for an n-point transform. However, the DCT has a higher compression efficiency since it avoids the generation of spurious spectral components. We now consider this phenomenon in more detail. The DFT is the discrete Fourier series representation of a finite-duration sequence, and as such, there is an implicit periodicity of the sequence as shown in Fig. 10.4a. This periodicity is the result of sampling in the frequency domain. Replicating the original sequence in this manner often creates severe discontinuities between the segments. These discontinuities result in spurious high frequency components that can considerably reduce the efficiency of the transform. Although these spurious components are not really part of the original sequence, they are required to reconstruct the sharp boundaries

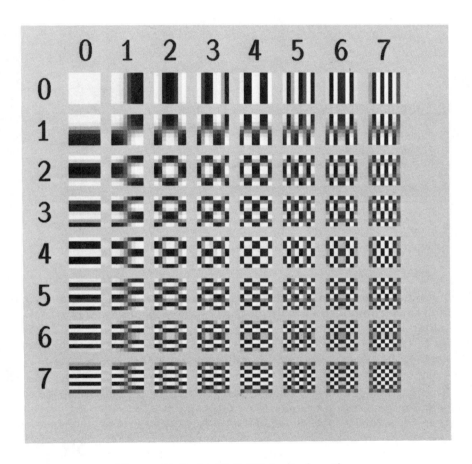

Figure 10.3: 8 × 8 DCT basis functions.

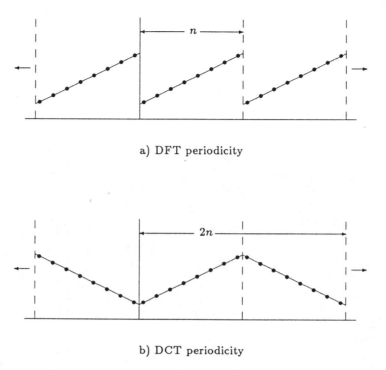

a) DFT periodicity

b) DCT periodicity

Figure 10.4: Implicit periodicities of the DFT and the DCT.

in the periodic sequence. Attempting to increase the transform efficiency by discarding these components results in objectionable reconstruction errors at the boundaries. In image coding, where the image is broken up into blocks of pixels to form 2-D sequences, these reconstruction errors result in blocking artifacts, i.e., the boundaries between adjacent blocks are highly visible.

To eliminate the boundary discontinuities, the original n-point sequence can be extended into a $2n$-point sequence by reflecting it about the vertical axis. The extended sequence is then repeated to form the periodic sequence required for the discrete Fourier series. As shown in Fig. 10.4b, this periodic sequence does not have any discontinuities at the boundaries, and no spurious spectral components are introduced in the DFT. It should be noted that the $2n$-point extended sequence is even symmetric (and real since we are processing pixel values), so the resulting $2n$-point DFT is also even symmetric (and real), and only n transform coefficients are required to represent it. Since we are dealing with real quantities in this case, the DFT requires only real computations. This process of taking the $2n$-point DFT of the extended n-point sequence is identical to the DCT of the original n-point sequence. In fact, the DCT can be computed as a $2n$-point FFT. While the DFT and DCT are intimately related, it is obvious that the symmetry implicit in the DCT results in two major advantages over the DFT. First, the DCT does not generate spurious spectral components, so coding efficiency remains high and blocking artifacts are greatly reduced, and second, only real computations are required for the DCT. Because of these advantages, DCT has become by far the most widely used transform for image compression.

10.3.4   Walsh-Hadamard transform (WHT)

Although the WHT is far from being optimal in an energy-packing sense for most imagery (as compared to the DCT), its modest decorrelating capability along with its simple implementation has made it popular, especially for hardware implementations. The WHT basis functions contain values that are either $+1$ or -1, and can be found from the rows of orthonormal Hadamard matrices [26]. The smallest orthonormal Hadamard matrix is of size 2×2:

$$\mathbf{H}_2 = \frac{1}{\sqrt{2}} \begin{bmatrix} 1 & 1 \\ 1 & -1 \end{bmatrix}. \tag{10.11}$$

Note the similarities between this matrix and the rotation matrices used in the example in Section 10.1. To construct larger Hadamard matrices, we can use the recursive relationship

$$\mathbf{H}_{2n} = \frac{1}{\sqrt{2}} \begin{bmatrix} \mathbf{H}_n & \mathbf{H}_n \\ \mathbf{H}_n & -\mathbf{H}_n \end{bmatrix}, \tag{10.12}$$

where $\mathbf{H}_{2n}$ is the Hadamard matrix of size $2n \times 2n$.

10.4   Transform Coding Strategies

A transform coding scheme generally uses an image-independent transform such as the DCT or WHT on 2-D blocks of an image and then employs a given strategy for the selection, quantization, and encoding of the transform coefficients. In the following, we provide a brief overview of two popular strategies and describe several variations within each general approach. We then elaborate on a particular DCT scheme that has been selected by the Joint Photographic Experts Group (JPEG) as the world standard for the compression of still-frame, continuous-tone, color images.

10.4.1   Zonal sample selection

In its simplest form, zonal sampling consists of retaining only those transform coefficients that are located in a prespecified zone in the transformed block and setting all other coefficients to zero. Since most images have a lowpass power spectrum, the lower frequency coefficients are generally retained while the higher frequency coefficients are discarded. Each retained coefficient is then quantized and encoded with a fixed-length codeword. It is possible to use the same quantizer for each coefficient, e.g., an 8-bit uniform quantizer, or to specify different quantizers for various groups of coefficients. For example, an 8-bit quantizer could be used for three lowest frequency coefficients, a 7-bit quantizer for the next five lowest frequency coefficients, etc. Since the selected sample locations and the quantizer(s) are both prespecified, no overhead information is required.

A more refined strategy involves allocating bits (out of a fixed total number) to the individual coefficients within the prespecified zone so as to minimize the total quantization error [30]. This is done by assigning bits in proportion to the logarithm of coefficient variances. The variance at each coefficient location is found by computing the corresponding coefficient energy in each block and then averaging over all image blocks. This approach requires two passes to encode the image. The first pass computes the coefficient variances and determines the appropriate quantizers. The quantizer information is transmitted to the receiver as overhead in the form of a bit-allocation matrix. The blocks are then actually encoded during the second pass.

In the technique just described, the bit-allocation matrix was computed based on global image statistics. Due to the nonstationary nature of images, there may be significant variations among the statistics of different blocks. Using the same bit-allocation matrix for all blocks can cause large errors when a coefficient value greatly deviates from its expected value. This problem is somewhat alleviated by using a locally adaptive version of the above strategy. In this approach, each block is classified into one of several classes and a different bit-allocation matrix is used for each class [31]. The classification is typically based on the total variance (energy) of the block since this is a good measure of the block activity. This scheme also requires two passes. During the first pass, the different classes are formed by computing the statistics of all image blocks. Usually, an equal number of blocks are assigned to each class. Then, the coefficient retention zone and the bit-allocation matrix for each class are determined and transmitted to the receiver. During the second pass, this information is used to classify each block and encode it according to its corresponding bit-allocation matrix.

The above schemes are aimed at encoding images at a constant bit rate. A lower, but variable, bit rate can be achieved if variable-length codes are employed. This is because the distributions of the coefficient amplitude values are generally nonuniform, e.g., Gaussian or Laplacian. As a result, the output levels of the quantizer exhibit a wide variation in their frequencies of occurrence and can be variable-length encoded to advantage. The reduction in bit rate can be particularly significant when the quantizer is uniform since the variations in the frequencies of occurrence will be greater than if a nonuniform quantizer is used. A global Huffman code can often be used since the relative symbol frequencies do not substantially change from image to image.

10.4.2 Threshold sample selection

A major drawback of the zonal sample selection strategy is that some of the coefficients outside the coefficient retention zone may contain significant energy and their omission can result in large reconstruction errors. To overcome this problem, a threshold sample selection process can be used where a threshold level is chosen and only the coefficients whose values are above the threshold are quantized and encoded [28]. Either uniform or nonuniform quantizers may be used. If a uniform quantizer is used, its output levels are usually entropy encoded [28].

A problem with threshold sample selection is that the addresses of the selected coefficients must be transmitted since the number and location of the coefficients that are above the threshold change from block to block. The techniques for encoding the addressing information are usually based on some variation of runlength encoding of the zero-valued, i.e., subthreshold, coefficients. A variation on the threshold sampling approach is to transmit the position and value of the L largest coefficients in each block [32]. The value of L may either be fixed or may vary depending on some attribute of the block such as its variance. To allow for more adaptivity, the number of quantizer levels can also vary depending on the activity of the block.

The quantizer structure can also be made a function of the coefficient location so as to control the amount of distortion introduced in each coefficient. To simplify the implementation, the various quantizers can be designed so that they differ only by a scaling factor. A single quantizer can then be used for all the coefficients, provided the coefficients are scaled (normalized) prior to quantization in order to achieve the desired step size. A useful method for determining the normalization for each coefficient is to make use of the HVS contrast sensitivity function. In this way, the quantization error for each coefficient can be made a function of that coefficient's perceptual importance.

The JPEG-proposed DCT algorithm [33] is essentially a threshold sample selection technique that allows a user-specified normalization array to be applied to the coefficients. There is actually no explicit threshold specified in this technique, but the use of a normalization array combined with the subsequent quantization effectively results in a thresholding process. In the next section we examine this algorithm in detail.

10.5 JPEG DCT Algorithm

The JPEG-proposed algorithm structure comprises three main components. The first is a baseline system that provides a simple and efficient algorithm that is adequate for most image coding applications. The second is a set of extended system features that allow the baseline system to satisfy a broader range of applications. Among these optional features are 12-bit/pixel input, progressive sequential and hierarchical build-up, and arithmetic coding. Finally, an independent lossless method is included for applications requiring that type of compression. The following section summarizes the main features of the baseline system that is the heart of the JPEG standard. For more information, one is referred to the JPEG proposal [33], which includes the complete description and details of the different algorithm components.

10.5.1   JPEG baseline system

The following is a brief description of the JPEG baseline system.

- The original image is partitioned into 8×8 pixel blocks and each block is independently transformed using the DCT.

- All transform coefficients are normalized (weighted) by applying a user-defined normalization array that is fixed for all blocks. Each component of the normalization array is an 8-bit integer and is passed to the receiver as part of the header information that is required for every image. Up to four different normalization arrays can be specified; e.g., different normalization arrays may be used for the different color components of a color image. The normalized coefficients are then uniformly quantized by rounding to the nearest integer. The normalization array can be viewed as scaling the quantizer so as to control the amount of quantization error introduced in each coefficient. The HVS contrast sensitivity function can be used as a guide in developing a normalization array that weighs each coefficient according to its perceptual importance.

- The top-left coefficient in the 2-D DCT array is referred to as the DC coefficient and is proportional to the average brightness of the spatial block. After quantization, this coefficient is encoded with a lossless DPCM scheme using the quantized DC coefficient from the previous block as a 1-D predictor. For the baseline system, up to two separate Huffman tables for encoding the resulting differential signal can be specified in the header information.

- The quantization of the AC coefficients produces many zeros, especially at higher frequencies. To take advantage of these zeros, the 2-D array of the DCT coefficients is formatted into a 1-D vector using a zigzag reordering. This rearranges the coefficients in approximately decreasing order of their average energy (as well as in order of increasing spatial frequency) with the aim of creating large runs of zero values.

- To encode the AC coefficients, each nonzero coefficient is first described by a composite 8-bit value $(0 \rightarrow 255)$, denoted by I, of the form (in binary notation):

$$I = \text{'NNNNSSSS'.}$$

The four least significant bits, 'SSSS', define a category for the coefficient amplitude. The values in category k are in the range $(2^{k-1}, 2^k - 1)$ or $(-2^k + 1, -2^{k-1})$, where $1 \leq k \leq 10$ for the baseline system. The coefficient values contained in each category are shown in Table 10.1. Given the category, it is then necessary to send an additional k bits to completely specify the sign and magnitude of a coefficient within that category. The four most significant bits in the composite value, 'NNNN', give the position of the current coefficient relative to the previous nonzero coefficient, i.e., the runlength of zero coefficients between nonzero coefficients. The runlengths specified by 'NNNN' can range from 0 to 15, and a separate symbol, $I = \text{'11110000'}$ (binary) $= 240$, is defined to represent a runlength of 16 zero coefficients. If the runlength exceeds 16 zero coefficients, it is coded by using multiple symbols. In addition, a special symbol, $I = 0$, is used to code the end of block (EOB), which signals that all the remaining coefficients in the block are zero. Therefore, the total symbol set contains 162 members (10 categories $\times$ 16 runlength values $+$ 2 additional symbols). The output symbols for each block are then Huffman coded and are followed by the additional bits (assumed to be uniformly distributed and thus fixed-length coded) required to specify the sign and exact magnitude of the coefficient in each of the categories. Up to two separate Huffman tables for the AC coefficients can be specified in the baseline system.

Category	AC Coefficient Range
1	$-1, 1$
2	$-3, -2, 2, 3$
3	$-7, \cdots, -4, 4, \cdots, 7$
4	$-15, \cdots, -8, 8, \cdots, 15$
5	$-31, \cdots, -16, 16, \cdots, 31$
6	$-63, \cdots, -32, 32, \cdots, 63$
7	$-127, \cdots, -64, 64, \cdots, 127$
8	$-255, \cdots, -128, 128, \cdots, 255$
9	$-511, \cdots, -256, 256, \cdots, 511$
10	$-1023, \cdots, -512, 512, \cdots, 1023$

Table 10.1: AC coefficient grouping.

- Each component of a color (or multispectral) image is encoded independently. For example, an image represented in the YIQ space (refer to Appendix A: Compression of Color Images) is encoded essentially as three separate images.

- At the decoder, after the encoded bit stream is Huffman decoded and the 2-D array of quantized DCT coefficients is recovered, each coefficient is denormalized by multiplying it by the corresponding component of the normalization matrix. The resultant array is inverse DCT-transformed to yield an approximation to the original image block. The resulting reconstruction error depends on the amount of quantization, which is controlled by the normalization matrix.

10.5.2   JPEG DCT example

In the following example, we further illustrate the different steps involved in the encoding of a block using the JPEG baseline system. Consider the following 8×8 block of pixel values from the LENA image:

$$
f(j,k) = \begin{bmatrix}
139 & 144 & 149 & 153 & 155 & 155 & 155 & 155 \\
144 & 151 & 153 & 156 & 159 & 156 & 156 & 156 \\
150 & 155 & 160 & 163 & 158 & 156 & 156 & 156 \\
159 & 161 & 162 & 160 & 160 & 159 & 159 & 159 \\
159 & 160 & 161 & 162 & 162 & 155 & 155 & 155 \\
161 & 161 & 161 & 161 & 160 & 157 & 157 & 157 \\
162 & 162 & 161 & 163 & 162 & 157 & 157 & 157 \\
162 & 162 & 161 & 161 & 163 & 158 & 158 & 158
\end{bmatrix}.
$$

The JPEG system actually uses a slightly different DCT than is given in Eq. (10.8). The forward JPEG DCT is defined as

$$
F(u,v) = \frac{C(u)C(v)}{4} \sum_{j=0}^{7} \sum_{k=0}^{7} f(j,k) \, \cos\left[\frac{(2j+1)u\pi}{16}\right] \cos\left[\frac{(2k+1)v\pi}{16}\right].
$$

$$(10.13)$$

Equation (10.13) is identical to Eq. (10.8) for $n = 8$ except for a scaling factor of 4. It is interesting to note that this scaling results in a distance-preserving forward transform, whereas Eq. (10.8) does not. The scaling of the inverse transform is adjusted accordingly. To reduce the hardware and software complexity, several implementations of Eq. (10.13) have been developed with the aim of minimizing the number of multiplications and additions. These practical DCT algorithms all use fixed-precision integer arithmetic. Using Eq. (10.13) with the integer arithmetic implementation given in [34], the transformed block for our example is given by

$$
F(u, v) = \begin{bmatrix}
1260 & -1 & -12 & -5 & 2 & -2 & -3 & 1 \\
-23 & -17 & -6 & -3 & -3 & 0 & 0 & -1 \\
-11 & -9 & -2 & 2 & 0 & -1 & -1 & 0 \\
-7 & -2 & 0 & 1 & 1 & 0 & 0 & 0 \\
-1 & -1 & 1 & 2 & 0 & -1 & 1 & 1 \\
2 & 0 & 2 & 0 & -1 & 1 & 1 & -1 \\
-1 & 0 & 0 & -1 & 0 & 2 & 1 & -1 \\
-3 & 2 & -4 & -2 & 2 & 1 & -1 & 0
\end{bmatrix}.
$$

The top-left transform coefficient is 8 times the average brightness (DC value) of the block, and it can be seen that the energy of the block is concentrated in only a few low-frequency coefficients. The DCT coefficients are then normalized and quantized using a user-defined normalization array that is fixed for all blocks. Each component of the normalization array, $Q(u, v)$, is an 8-bit integer that in effect determines the quantization step size; larger values correspond to larger quantization steps. The bit rate of an encoded image can be varied by changing this array, e.g., by scaling it by a constant factor. A typical normalization array that has been used by JPEG in their studies is

$$
Q(u, v) = \begin{bmatrix}
16 & 11 & 10 & 16 & 24 & 40 & 51 & 61 \\
12 & 12 & 14 & 19 & 26 & 58 & 60 & 55 \\
14 & 13 & 16 & 24 & 40 & 57 & 69 & 56 \\
14 & 17 & 22 & 29 & 51 & 87 & 80 & 62 \\
18 & 22 & 37 & 56 & 68 & 109 & 103 & 77 \\
24 & 35 & 55 & 64 & 81 & 104 & 113 & 92 \\
49 & 64 & 78 & 87 & 103 & 121 & 120 & 101 \\
72 & 92 & 95 & 98 & 112 & 100 & 103 & 99
\end{bmatrix}.
$$

The resulting normalized and quantized coefficient, $F^*(u, v)$, is given by

$$
F^*(u, v) = \text{Nearest integer} \left(\frac{F(u, v)}{Q(u, v)} \right) \approx \left\lfloor \frac{F(u, v) + \lfloor \frac{Q(u,v)}{2} \rfloor}{Q(u, v)} \right\rfloor, \quad (10.14)
$$

where $\lfloor x \rfloor$ denotes the largest integer smaller than x. Quantizing the integer-DCT array in the example according to this rule results in

$$F^*(u,v) = \begin{bmatrix} 79 & 0 & -1 & 0 & 0 & 0 & 0 & 0 \\ -2 & -1 & 0 & 0 & 0 & 0 & 0 & 0 \\ -1 & -1 & 0 & 0 & 0 & 0 & 0 & 0 \\ 0 & 0 & 0 & 0 & 0 & 0 & 0 & 0 \\ 0 & 0 & 0 & 0 & 0 & 0 & 0 & 0 \\ 0 & 0 & 0 & 0 & 0 & 0 & 0 & 0 \\ 0 & 0 & 0 & 0 & 0 & 0 & 0 & 0 \\ 0 & 0 & 0 & 0 & 0 & 0 & 0 & 0 \end{bmatrix}.$$

Notice how the normalization and quantization process has produced many zero-valued coefficients. The quantized DCT coefficients are now reordered into a 1-D format using the following zigzag scan (ordered from $0 \rightarrow 63$):

$$\begin{bmatrix} 0 & 1 & 5 & 6 & 14 & 15 & 27 & 28 \\ 2 & 4 & 7 & 13 & 16 & 26 & 29 & 42 \\ 3 & 8 & 12 & 17 & 25 & 30 & 41 & 43 \\ 9 & 11 & 18 & 24 & 31 & 40 & 44 & 53 \\ 10 & 19 & 23 & 32 & 39 & 45 & 52 & 54 \\ 20 & 22 & 33 & 38 & 46 & 51 & 55 & 60 \\ 21 & 34 & 37 & 47 & 50 & 56 & 59 & 61 \\ 35 & 36 & 48 & 49 & 57 & 58 & 62 & 63 \end{bmatrix}.$$

For our example, this reordering results in

$$79 \quad 0 \quad -2 \quad -1 \quad -1 \quad -1 \quad 0 \quad 0 \quad -1 \quad \text{EOB}.$$

The DC value and AC coefficients in the 1-D sequence are encoded using separate local or global Huffman tables that are transmitted to the receiver as part of the header information. As described previously, instead of encoding the DC value directly, the difference between it and the DC value of the previous block is first formed and the result is encoded using the DC Huffman code table. The AC coefficients are encoded using a Huffman code table similar to the one given in Table 10.2. The AC Huffman code table contains the 162 symbols described in the previous section. The maximum allowable codeword length for each symbol is restricted to 16 bits and no codeword may consist of all 1's. In Table 10.2, we have only listed those symbols whose codeword length is smaller than 10 bits.

In our example sequence, the first nonzero AC coefficient has a value of -2. It is separated from the previous nonzero coefficient (in this case the DC coefficient) by a run of 1 zero. Referring to Table 10.1, we find that -2 falls

Zero Run	Category	Code length	Codeword
0	1	2	00
0	2	2	01
0	3	3	100
0	4	4	1011
0	5	5	11010
0	6	6	111000
0	7	7	1111000
.	.	.	.
.	.	.	.
1	1	4	1100
1	2	6	111001
1	3	7	1111001
1	4	9	111110110
.	.	.	.
.	.	.	.
2	1	5	11011
2	2	8	11111000
.	.	.	.
.	.	.	.
3	1	6	111010
3	2	9	111110111
.	.	.	.
.	.	.	.
4	1	6	111011
5	1	7	1111010
6	1	7	1111011
7	1	8	11111001
8	1	8	11111010
9	1	9	111111000
10	1	9	111111001
11	1	9	111111010
.	.	.	.
.	.	.	.
End of Block (EOB)		4	1010

Table 10.2: Example of JPEG AC Huffman code table.

into the category $k = 2$. From Table 10.2, a category 2 coefficient preceded by 1 zero is represented by the 6-bit Huffman codeword 111001. This codeword is then followed by a sign bit (0 for negative coefficients) and additional $k - 1$ bits to identify the magnitude of the coefficient within its category. Proceeding in this manner, the bit stream produced by concatenating the codewords is

DC difference Huffman codeword/11100101/000/000/000/110110/1010.

Assuming 8 bits are used for the DC difference Huffman codeword, a total of 35 bits are needed to encode the 8×8 block in the example. The resulting bit rate is 35 bits/64 pixels = 0.55 bit/pixel. At the receiver, the quantized coefficients are reconstructed by the Huffman decoding procedure and are then denormalized according to

$$\hat{F}(u, v) = F^*(u, v)Q(u, v). \tag{10.15}$$

The denormalized block is then inverse transformed using an integer DCT as in [34]. The reconstructed block is

$$\hat{f}(j, k) = \begin{bmatrix} 144 & 146 & 149 & 152 & 154 & 156 & 156 & 156 \\ 148 & 150 & 152 & 154 & 156 & 156 & 156 & 156 \\ 155 & 156 & 157 & 158 & 158 & 157 & 156 & 155 \\ 160 & 161 & 161 & 162 & 161 & 159 & 157 & 155 \\ 163 & 163 & 164 & 163 & 162 & 160 & 158 & 156 \\ 163 & 163 & 164 & 164 & 162 & 160 & 158 & 157 \\ 160 & 161 & 162 & 162 & 162 & 161 & 159 & 158 \\ 158 & 159 & 161 & 161 & 162 & 161 & 159 & 158 \end{bmatrix}.$$

The errors introduced in the code values of the original image block due to compression are

$$e(j, k) = \begin{bmatrix} -5 & -2 & 0 & 1 & 1 & -1 & -1 & -1 \\ -4 & 1 & 1 & 2 & 3 & 0 & 0 & 0 \\ -5 & -1 & 3 & 5 & 0 & -1 & 0 & 1 \\ -1 & 0 & 1 & -2 & -1 & 0 & 2 & 4 \\ -4 & -3 & -3 & -1 & 0 & -5 & -3 & -1 \\ -2 & -2 & -3 & -3 & -2 & -3 & -1 & 0 \\ 2 & 1 & -1 & 1 & 0 & -4 & -2 & -1 \\ 4 & 3 & 0 & 0 & 1 & -3 & -1 & 0 \end{bmatrix},$$

where $e(j, k) = f(j, k) - \hat{f}(j, k)$. The RMSE resulting from the encoding of this block is

$$\text{RMSE} = \sqrt{\frac{1}{64} \sum_{j=0}^{7} \sum_{k=0}^{7} e^2(j, k)} = 2.26.$$

10.6 JPEG DCT Results

The results of applying the JPEG DCT algorithm are summarized in Table 10.3 for the two test images. The bit rate was set to 0.25, 0.50, 0.75, 1.00, and 1.50 bits/pixel by varying the normalization array scaling. Figures 10.5 - 10.9 are the reconstructed and error images for LENA at these bit rates. Figure 10.10 shows a magnified section of LENA to illustrate the performance and artifacts of the JPEG DCT algorithm at 0.50 bit/pixel.

Technique	Bit rate bits/pixel	LENA		BOOTS	
		RMSE (0-255)	SNR (dB)	RMSE (0-255)	SNR (dB)
JPEG DCT	0.25	7.34	30.81	14.78	24.73
JPEG DCT	0.50	4.70	34.69	10.07	28.07
JPEG DCT	0.75	3.78	36.58	8.20	29.85
JPEG DCT	1.00	3.23	37.93	6.92	31.33
JPEG DCT	1.50	2.56	39.95	5.02	34.12

Table 10.3: DCT results.

10.7 Implementation Issues and Complexity of JPEG DCT Algorithm

As with all memoryless block processing techniques, the DCT algorithm is amenable to parallel processing. However, sequential processing is assumed in the following discussion. The major contributor to the complexity of the algorithm is, of course, the forward or inverse DCT computation. There are two common approaches to the 2-D DCT computation [35]. One approach is to use the separability property to compute a $n \times n$ 2-D DCT as $2n$ 1-D DCTs of size n. The other approach is to directly compute the full 2-D transform. Although the latter can result in a smaller number of operations per block [36], we will only consider the separable approach since it has a simpler structure and is more amenable to hardware implementations.

Several well-known algorithms [37,38] require 29 additions and 13 multiplications to perform an 8-point 1-D DCT as defined in Eq. (10.8). However, in the context of the JPEG DCT algorithm, a scaled version of the DCT (where each coefficient might have a different scaling) is used, and any scalings required in computing the basic DCT can be easily incorporated by modifying the normalization array. For a 1-D DCT of length 8, this can further reduce the required number of multiplications to 5 [39]. A total of 16 1-D DCTs are needed to process each 8×8 block, and consequently, a total of 464 additions and 80 multiplications are required per block. According to Eq. (10.14), the normalization and quantization of each coefficient can be done with one addition and one multiplication (division). This process may be bypassed if a coefficient magnitude, $|F(u, v)|$, is less than $\lfloor \frac{Q(u,v)}{2} \rfloor$, since it would be quantized to zero. Since the quantization process generally creates a large fraction of zero coefficients (an average of at least 80% at typical bit rates), bypassing the normalization and quantization step can result in significant savings in a software implementation of the algorithm. The variable-length coding consists of one comparison per coefficient to identify the nonzero coefficients and one addition per coefficient (worst case) to update the register, which counts the runlength of zero coefficients. The actual Huffman encoding is performed using a table look-up and would involve additional operations for data management (bit packing) in software. Therefore, ignoring the complexity of the Huffman encoding and considering a full multiply for the quantization process, the encoder requires a total of

- 2.25 multiplications,

- 9.25 additions, and

- 1 comparison

per pixel. The decoder is similar to the encoder except that the Huffman decoding is slightly more complex than the encoding. A minimal amount of permanent memory is required to store the Huffman code tables and the HVS normalization array(s). Also, working memory is required to store the lines of the input pixels needed to form the blocks.

The effects of a channel error are catastrophic because of the Huffman coding, and JPEG has made detailed provisions for resynchronization codes. For DCT schemes that do not use variable-length coding, the effects of a channel error are limited to a single block. The impact of the error will vary depending on which coefficients have been affected. If a low-order coefficient is incorrect, the block error may be quite objectionable, e.g., a basis function becomes apparent or the overall block mean is incorrect, while errors in the higher order coefficients may not be as noticeable.

Figure 10.5: JPEG DCT at 0.25 bit/pixel.

Figure 10.6: JPEG DCT at 0.50 bit/pixel.

Figure 10.7: JPEG DCT at 0.75 bit/pixel.

Figure 10.8: JPEG DCT at 1.00 bit/pixel.

Figure 10.9: JPEG DCT at 1.50 bits/pixel.

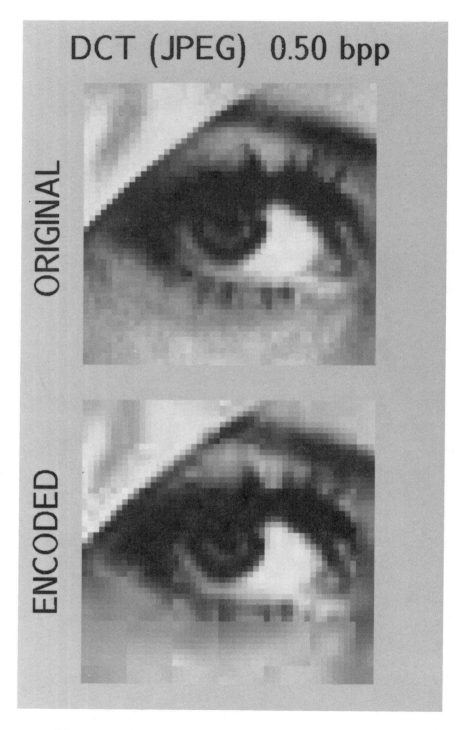

Figure 10.10: JPEG DCT at 0.50 bit/pixel (magnified).

Chapter 11

Block Truncation Coding

In *block truncation coding* (BTC), an image is segmented into $n \times n$ (typically, 4×4) nonoverlapping blocks of pixels, and a two-level (one-bit) quantizer is independently designed for each block. Both the quantizer threshold and the two reconstruction levels are varied in response to the local statistics of a block. Thus, encoding is essentially a local binarization process, and the representation of a block consists of an $n \times n$ bit map indicating the reconstruction level associated with each pixel and overhead information specifying the two reconstruction levels. Decoding is the simple process of placing the appropriate reconstruction value at each pixel location as per the bit map. A diagram of the basic BTC scheme is shown in Fig. 11.1.

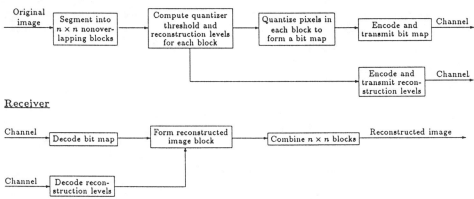

Figure 11.1: BTC block diagram.

As an example of block truncation coding, consider the following 4×4 block of pixels containing a noisy diagonal edge:

$$\mathbf{X} = \begin{bmatrix} 146 & 149 & 152 & 156 \\ 97 & 122 & 144 & 147 \\ 89 & 90 & 135 & 145 \\ 85 & 92 & 99 & 120 \end{bmatrix}.$$

In this example, we design the quantizer so that the threshold is the mean, $\overline{X}$, of the entire block, and the two reconstruction levels, a and b, are the means of the segments determined by the threshold. For this block of pixels, $\overline{X} = 123.0$, and using this as the threshold, the bit map is

$$\mathbf{B} = \begin{bmatrix} 1 & 1 & 1 & 1 \\ 0 & 0 & 1 & 1 \\ 0 & 0 & 1 & 1 \\ 0 & 0 & 0 & 0 \end{bmatrix},$$

where 1 indicates that the actual pixel value is greater than the threshold and 0 indicates that it is below the threshold. Computing the mean of each segment and rounding to the nearest integer, we find that the two reconstruction values are $a = 99$ and $b = 147$. These values are transmitted along with the bit map, and the reconstructed block is

$$\hat{\mathbf{X}} = \begin{bmatrix} 147 & 147 & 147 & 147 \\ 99 & 99 & 147 & 147 \\ 99 & 99 & 147 & 147 \\ 99 & 99 & 99 & 99 \end{bmatrix}.$$

If we assume that the reconstruction levels are represented by 8 bits each and no additional source coding is used on the bit map, the total bit rate is $(8 + 8 + 16)/16 = 2.0$ bits/pixel.

In this example, it can be seen that a distinct jaggedness has been introduced in the noisy edge by the thresholding process and by the restriction to only two reconstruction levels within the block. This basic design of BTC can also cause contouring artifacts in slowly varying blocks because of abrupt changes in the reconstruction value. Other artifacts can result from the independent processing of each block and are manifested as a lack of edge continuity between adjacent blocks or an abrupt change in the reconstruction value at a block boundary. On the positive side, the thresholding process in BTC makes it possible to reproduce a sharp edge with high fidelity, while other compression schemes typically blur sharp edges.

In the following sections, the key elements in a BTC system are discussed further, namely,

- design of the quantizer and

- additional source coding of the bit map and the reconstruction levels to reduce the bit rate.

11.1 Quantizer Design

In the example, the quantizer was designed based on local mean values. As we shall see, this quantizer preserves the first and second absolute moments of the block and also minimizes the mean-squared reconstruction error when the threshold is restricted to the block mean. It is also possible to use other criteria in developing the quantizer, and it is not necessary to restrict the threshold to the block mean. Since a BTC quantizer is specified by a threshold and two reconstruction levels, we have three degrees of freedom to use in the design of the quantizer. We can thus impose a maximum of three constraints, e.g., constrain the threshold to be the mean of the block and constrain the reconstruction values to preserve the first two absolute moments. In the following sections, we discuss two common approaches to BTC quantizer design: moment preservation and error minimization.

11.1.1 Moment-preserving quantizers

Many of the BTC schemes reported in the literature make use of *moment-preserving* (MP) quantizers [40-48]. These are quantizers that preserve a limited number of moments over a block, e.g., the block mean and variance. The rationale for this approach is that by preserving moments, important visual information is being retained, namely, central tendency (mean) and dispersion or busyness about the mean (variance). The three degrees of freedom inherent in a BTC quantizer allow a maximum of three moments to be matched, e.g., mean, variance, and skewness, or a set of three higher order moments [41-45]. Although MP quantizers are generally nonparametric in that no assumptions are made about the probability density function of the pixels in each block, it is possible to develop parametric MP quantizers [41].

The earliest reported work on BTC presented a quantizer designed to preserve the block mean and variance [40]. The image is first divided into nonoverlapping $n \times n$ blocks. Let $m = n^2$, and let $X_1, X_2, \ldots, X_m$ be the pixel values in a given block of the original image. The quantities we wish to preserve are the first and second sample moments:

$$\overline{X} = \frac{1}{m} \sum_{i=1}^{m} X_i, \tag{11.1}$$

$$\overline{X^2} = \frac{1}{m} \sum_{i=1}^{m} X_i^2. \tag{11.2}$$

The variance is given by

$$\sigma^2 = \overline{X^2} - \overline{X}^2, \tag{11.3}$$

and thus if $\overline{X}$ and $\overline{X^2}$ are preserved, the variance is also preserved. It is now necessary to find a threshold X_{th} and two reconstruction levels, a and b, such that

$$\hat{X}_i = \begin{cases} a, & \text{if } X_i < X_{th} \\ b, & \text{if } X_i \geq X_{th} \end{cases} \tag{11.4}$$
$$\text{for } i = 1, 2, \ldots, m.$$

Since we wish to preserve the first two sample moments, two degrees of freedom are required, which can be provided by the two reconstruction levels. The remaining degree of freedom is used by setting the threshold to $\overline{X}$ to simplify the analysis. Let q be the number of X_i's greater than or equal to the threshold $\overline{X}$. To preserve $\overline{X}$ and $\overline{X^2}$ we must satisfy

$$m\overline{X} = (m - q)\, a + q\, b, \tag{11.5}$$
$$m\overline{X^2} = (m - q)\, a^2 + q\, b^2. \tag{11.6}$$

Solving for a and b yields

$$a = \overline{X} - \sigma \sqrt{\frac{q}{m - q}}, \tag{11.7}$$

$$b = \overline{X} + \sigma \sqrt{\frac{m - q}{q}}. \tag{11.8}$$

We transmit the $n \times n$ bit map indicating which pixels reconstruct to a and which reconstruct to b as well as information specifying a and b. It is possible to transmit a and b directly (typically using 8 bits for each) or to send $\overline{X}$ and σ instead since a and b can be computed from them using Eqs. (11.7) and (11.8). (Note that q is known from the bit map.) The advantage in the latter approach is that $\overline{X}$ and σ are more amenable than a and b to *joint quantization* techniques, and they can be encoded using a reduced number of bits [42,46,47]. This approach is described in more detail in Section 11.2 on source encoding techniques for BTC.

One disadvantage in a hardware implementation of this quantizer is that squaring and square root operations are required. An approach that eliminates these operations, yet offers similar performance, is *absolute moment block truncation coding* (AMBTC) in which the quantizer is designed to preserve absolute moments [48]. The mean and the first absolute central moment of an $n \times n$ $(m = n^2)$ block are given respectively by

$$\overline{X} = \frac{1}{m} \sum_{i=1}^{m} X_i, \tag{11.9}$$

$$\alpha = \frac{1}{m} \sum_{i=1}^{m} |X_i - \overline{X}|. \tag{11.10}$$

If we again restrict the quantizer threshold to $\overline{X}$, the reconstruction levels needed to preserve $\overline{X}$ and α are

$$a = \overline{X} - \frac{m\alpha}{2(m-q)}, \tag{11.11}$$

$$b = \overline{X} + \frac{m\alpha}{2q}, \tag{11.12}$$

where q is the number of X_i's $\geq \overline{X}$. As in the previous technique, a and b can be encoded directly, or $\overline{X}$ and α can be encoded using joint quantization to reduce the bit rate. It is worthwhile noting that the computations for α can be simplified by using

$$\alpha = \frac{2}{m} \left[\sum_{\forall X_i \geq \overline{X}} X_i - q\,\overline{X} \right]. \tag{11.13}$$

This eliminates the absolute value operation in Eq. (11.10); a derivation for this is given in [48].

11.1.2   Error-minimizing quantizers

The performance of the absolute moment quantizer in terms of MSE is comparable to or slightly better than the performance of the quantizer that preserves the mean and variance. This is expected since the absolute moment quantizer is also the minimum MSE (MMSE) quantizer when the threshold is restricted to the mean. To show this, we start with the MSE for a given block:

$$\text{MSE} = \frac{1}{m} \left[\sum_{\forall X_i < \overline{X}} (X_i - a)^2 + \sum_{\forall X_i \geq \overline{X}} (X_i - b)^2 \right]. \tag{11.14}$$

Taking the partial derivative with respect to a, setting the result equal to zero, and solving for a yields

$$a = \frac{1}{(m-q)} \sum_{\forall X_i < \overline{X}} X_i. \tag{11.15}$$

Similar computations for b yield

$$b = \frac{1}{q} \sum_{\forall X_i \geq \overline{X}} X_i. \tag{11.16}$$

These reconstruction levels are merely the means of the two segments determined by the threshold $\overline{X}$. (Recall that this was used in our numerical example.) These expressions can also be generalized for an arbitrary threshold, but it then becomes necessary to search through all possible thresholds (at most, $m - 1$ thresholds) to find the one that yields the lowest overall MSE.

To see that using the conditional means for a and b is equivalent to the absolute moment quantizer, we can substitute Eq. (11.16) directly into Eq. (11.13) and rearrange to yield the expression for b given in Eq. (11.12). Using the relationship

$$\overline{X} = \frac{1}{m} \left[\sum_{\forall X_i < \overline{X}} X_i + \sum_{\forall X_i \geq \overline{X}} X_i \right] \tag{11.17}$$

with Eq. (11.15) in Eq. (11.13) similarly yields the expression for a given in Eq. (11.11).

11.2   Source Coding of Bit Map and Reconstruction Levels

BTC techniques typically operate on 4×4 blocks, so if 8 bits each are used for a and b and 16 bits are required for the bit map, the resulting bit rate is 2.0 bits/pixel. A number of source coding techniques can be employed on both the reconstruction levels and the bit map to reduce this bit rate. The price to be paid is generally an increase in the complexity of the algorithm and/or a decrease (often negligible) in reconstructed image quality.

11.2.1 Reduced bit representation/joint quantization

A simple technique to reduce the bit rate is to use less than 8 bits for each reconstruction level, but this generally results in lower image quality. However, if $\overline{X}$ and σ (or α) are transmitted instead of a and b, it is possible to use less than 8 bits each for $\overline{X}$ and σ without significantly degrading quality. Results presented in [42] and [48] indicate that using 6 bits for $\overline{X}$ and 4 bits for σ or α result in very little quality loss. Assuming no bit map encoding, this results in 1.63 bits/pixel for a 4×4 block.

A more sophisticated approach is joint (two-dimensional) quantization of $\overline{X}$ and σ (or $\overline{X}$ and α) [42,46]. The motivation for this approach is that the exact value of the mean is not critical in a high variance area, but it is critical in a low variance area. Thus $\overline{X}$ is coarsely quantized when σ or α is large and more finely quantized when they are small. Using this technique, $\overline{X}$ and σ or α can be jointly quantized using 10 bits for a bit rate of 1.63 bits/pixel with somewhat better performance than using independent quantization with 10 bits [42]. As an example of joint quantization, consider Table 11.1, which shows the allowed combinations of $\overline{X}$ and σ for a 6-bit (64 possible combinations) joint quantization scheme [46]. The original data contain 16 levels, so $\overline{X}$ ranges from 0 - 15. To use this table, σ is first quantized to the nearest value allowed in the table (0 - 7). Then, $\overline{X}$ is quantized to the nearest value from the set of $\overline{X}$'s allowed for the given σ. The 6-bit codeword associated with this combination of quantized $\overline{X}$ and σ values is transmitted and is used as an address to a similar lookup table at the receiver.

σ	$\overline{X}$	Number of codes
0	0-15	16
1	1-14	14
2	1,3,5,7,9,11,13,15	8
3	2,4,6,8,10,12,14	7
4	2,4,6,8,10,12,14	7
5	2,5,8,11,14	5
6	3,6,9,12	4
7	4,7,10	3
		Total = 64

Table 11.1: 6-bit joint quantization for $\overline{X}$ and σ.

11.2.2   Vector quantization encoding of reconstruction levels

Vector quantization (VQ) is another approach to encoding the reconstruction levels [49], and it is quite similar to the joint quantization approach. In the VQ approach, the lower reconstruction level, a, and the block mean, $\overline{X}$, are considered as a two-dimensional vector $[a, \overline{X}]$. We know that a will always be lower than or equal to $\overline{X}$, and we expect a to be high when $\overline{X}$ is high. Therefore, the set of vectors representing the blocks in an image typically occupy a limited region of the full 2-D space, and it should be possible to determine a limited set of reproduction vectors (the codebook) that adequately represents the original vectors. (For a more complete discussion on VQ, refer to Chapter 12.) In [49], a codebook containing 256 entries (8 bits) was generated using a training set of vectors. Images encoded with this method reportedly demonstrated good reconstruction quality at 1.5 bits/pixel.

11.2.3   Bit map omission

A very simple technique to reduce the bit rate is to omit transmission of the bit map if the variance of a block is small, or equivalently, if a and b differ by only a small amount [40]. For these cases, it is only necessary to transmit $\overline{X}$ as the reconstruction level for the entire block. Of course, the average bit rate achieved by this technique is highly dependent on the image being encoded, but for an image with large uniform areas, it results in a significant bit rate reduction with very little quality loss.

11.2.4   Independent/dependent bits

Another approach to bit map encoding is to denote certain locations in the bit map as independent bits and others as dependent bits [46,50]. Only the independent bits are transmitted, and the dependent bits are determined at the receiver using predefined logic. The choices for the particular independent and dependent bits and their logical relationships influence the type of structures that are preserved, e.g., horizontal lines, vertical lines, etc. Resulting quality with this method depends on these choices as well as the nature of the input image. The bit rate for this method is determined by the number of independent bits transmitted. For example, using 8 independent bits with a 4×4 block would reduce the nominal bit rate of 2.0 bits/pixel to 1.5 bits/pixel.

11.2.5 VQ encoding of bit map

The bit map can also be encoded with VQ in addition to the reconstruction levels as described previously [49]. For this method, the bit map is considered to be an m-dimensional vector consisting of 0's and 1's. For example, for a 4×4 block, we have a 16-dimensional vector of the form $[b_0, b_1, b_2, \ldots, b_{15}]$. A codebook is then generated using a training set of bit map vectors. In [49], a codebook containing 256 representative vectors (8 bits) was used, and reported results indicated good quality at 1.5 bits/pixel. Using VQ for both the bit map and the reconstruction levels resulted in somewhat lower image quality at 1.0 bit/pixel.

11.3 Adaptive Block Size BTC

BTC is inherently adaptive in terms of the quantizer design, and it can also be made adaptive in terms of the block size. Fixing the block size over the entire image is always a compromise. High activity regions require small blocks for accurate reconstruction while low activity regions can be easily encoded with large blocks. By allowing the block size to vary in response to local signal characteristics, reconstructed image quality can be improved at the possible expense of an increased bit rate.

The following steps summarize the encoder operation of an adaptive AMBTC algorithm that is a modification of the technique presented in [50]:

- The image is segmented into 4×4 blocks.

- The reconstruction levels, a and b, are calculated according to Eqs. (11.15) and (11.16).

- Each block is classified based on the resulting values of a and b. Three modes of operation are used:

<u>Mode A</u>: Given a suitable threshold T_1, then if

$$| a - b | \leq T_1, \tag{11.18}$$

skip the bit map and transmit only the average value of the 4×4 block. This mode is used in constant or relatively smooth areas that can be represented by a single gray level.

<u>Mode B</u>: Given suitable thresholds T_2 and T_3, then if

$$T_1 < | a - b | < T_2 \qquad \underline{\text{and}} \tag{11.19}$$

$$\left[\sum_{\forall X_i < \overline{X}} |X_i - a| \; + \; \sum_{\forall X_i \geq \overline{X}} |X_i - b| \right] \; \leq \; T_3, \qquad (11.20)$$

transmit both the reconstruction levels and the bit map of the 4×4 block. This is used in areas that can be accurately encoded by two gray levels. The threshold T_3 assures that the absolute reconstruction error is kept below that value.

<u>Mode C</u>: If none of the previous conditions are satisfied, segment the 4×4 block into 2×2 blocks and encode each 2×2 block using the AMBTC quantizer. Transmit both the bit map and the reconstruction levels for each 2×2 block. This mode is used in high activity regions where accurate encoding of the reconstruction levels is important.

- Overhead information is also transmitted for each block to indicate which mode has been selected.

Reconstruction quality is significantly improved over the fixed block size technique, but the bit rate will vary greatly depending on the activity in the image, as shown in the examples.

11.4   BTC Results

The results of applying the nonadaptive and adaptive AMBTC algorithms to the two test images are summarized in Table 11.2. The nonadaptive scheme used 4×4 blocks, and 8 bits each for the reconstruction levels a and b. No additional source coding was used, resulting in a bit rate of 2.0 bits/pixel. The adaptive technique switched between 4×4 and 2×2 blocks using the three modes described previously, and again, 8 bits were used for each reconstruction level with no additional source coding. The thresholds were $T_1 = 1, T_2 = 20$, and $T_3 = 60$. The corresponding probabilities of occurrence of the modes were $(0.004, 0.740, 0.256)$ for LENA and $(0.015, 0.459, 0.526)$ for BOOTS, resulting in bit rates of 2.89 and 3.68 bits/pixel, respectively. The overhead information needed to identify the mode is included in these bit rates (2 bits per 4×4 block).

Reconstructed and error images for LENA are shown in Figs. 11.2 and 11.3 for both the nonadaptive and adaptive techniques. A magnified section of the reconstructed image using nonadaptive AMBTC is shown in Fig. 11.4. The two reconstruction levels available in each 4×4 block should be apparent in this figure.

Technique	Bit rate bits/pixel	LENA		BOOTS	
		RMSE (0-255)	SNR (dB)	RMSE (0-255)	SNR (dB)
AMBTC	2.00	5.57	33.22	9.48	28.59
Adaptive AMBTC	2.89	3.05	38.46	—	—
	3.68	—	—	4.76	34.58

Table 11.2: BTC results.

11.5 Implementation Issues and Complexity of Adaptive Block Size AMBTC Algorithm

Since the AMBTC algorithm is a memoryless block processing technique, it is highly amenable to parallel processing. However, this aspect is not considered in the following discussion. For encoding each 4×4 block, computation of the mean requires 15 additions and 1 multiplication,[1] the bit map requires 16 comparisons, and the reconstruction levels require 14 additions and 2 multiplications. The mode A threshold test requires 1 addition and 1 comparison. If mode A is not selected, then the mode B threshold test is performed, requiring 31 additions and 2 comparisons. If mode B is not selected, then block truncation coding is performed on 2×2 blocks within the 4×4 blocks at a total computational cost of 20 additions, 12 multiplications, and 16 comparisons for the 4×4 block. For a best case scenario where only mode A is used, this results in

- 0.19 multiplications,

- 1.81 additions, and

- 1.06 comparisons

per pixel. In a worst case scenario, all modes are checked and mode C is always used. This results in

- 0.94 multiplications,

- 5.06 additions, and

- 2.19 comparisons

---

[1]The multiplication may be replaced by four logical shifts to the right since the multiplier is power of two.

per pixel. Decoding is extremely simple since it is only necessary to map the appropriate reconstruction value to each pixel. Memory requirements are also minimal for the adaptive AMBTC algorithm. Permanent memory is required only to store the thresholds, and the block processing nature of the algorithm necessitates only enough working memory to store the lines of input pixels needed to form the blocks. Also, memory is required to store any intermediate results prior to the selection of the appropriate mode.

Channel errors typically have a limited effect on reconstruction quality because of the block processing nature of BTC. Reconstruction errors are usually confined to a single block (either 4×4 or 2×2).

Figure 11.2: Nonadaptive AMBTC at 2.00 bits/pixel.

Figure 11.3: Adaptive AMBTC at 2.89 bits/pixel.

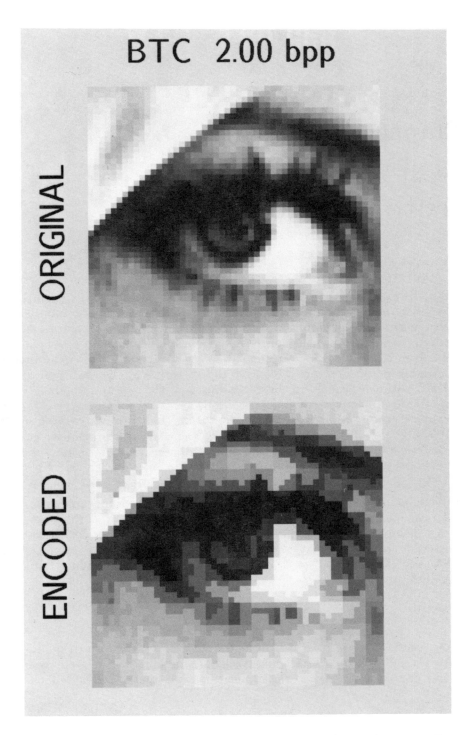

Figure 11.4: Nonadaptive AMBTC at 2.00 bits/pixel (magnified).

Chapter 12

Vector Quantization

In *vector quantization* (VQ), the original image is first decomposed into n-dimensional *image vectors*. The vectors can be generated in a number of different ways. For example, an $n = l \times m$ block of pixel values can be ordered to form an n-dimensional vector, or a 3-dimensional vector can be formed from the RGB color components of an individual pixel. The image may also be modified prior to forming the vectors, e.g., by the application of a DCT with the transform coefficients used as the vector components.

Each image vector, $\mathbf{X}$, is then compared with a collection of representative templates or *codevectors*, $\hat{\mathbf{X}}_i, i = 1, \ldots, N_c$, taken from a previously generated *codebook*.[1] The codevectors are also of dimension n. The best match codevector is chosen using a minimum distortion rule; i.e., choose $\hat{\mathbf{X}}_k$ such that $d(\mathbf{X}, \hat{\mathbf{X}}_k) \leq d(\mathbf{X}, \hat{\mathbf{X}}_j)$ for all $j = 1, \ldots, N_c$, where $d(\mathbf{X}, \hat{\mathbf{X}})$ denotes the distortion incurred in replacing the original vector $\mathbf{X}$ with the codevector $\hat{\mathbf{X}}$. Ideally, the distortion measure should be mathematically tractable and subjectively meaningful so that the quantitative distortion values correspond to perceived quality. The most common distortion measure used in image VQ is MSE, which corresponds to the square of the Euclidean distance between the two vectors; i.e.,

$$d(\mathbf{X}, \hat{\mathbf{X}}) = \frac{1}{n} \sum_{i=1}^{n} (x_i - \hat{x}_i)^2. \tag{12.1}$$

Although MSE does not necessarily correlate well with perceived quality, it is widely used because of its computational simplicity. A related measure that has proven useful in certain applications is weighted MSE, defined as

$$d_w(\mathbf{X}, \hat{\mathbf{X}}) = \frac{1}{n} \sum_{i=1}^{n} w_i \, (x_i - \hat{x}_i)^2, \tag{12.2}$$

---

[1] We use boldface notation, e.g., $\mathbf{X}$, to indicate vectors, where $\mathbf{X} = [x_1, x_2, \ldots, x_n]$ and the individual x_i's are the components of the vector.

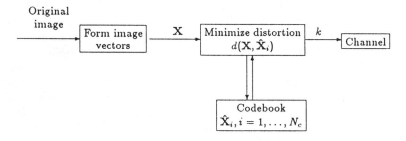

Transmitter

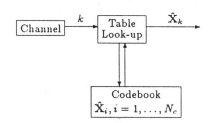

Receiver

Figure 12.1: VQ block diagram.

where the w_i's are the weighting factors applied to the vector component differences.

After a minimum distortion codevector has been selected, its index k is transmitted using $\log_2 N_c$ bits. At the receiver, this index is used as an entry to a duplicate codebook (a look-up table) to reproduce $\hat{\mathbf{X}}_k$. The VQ decoder has a very simple structure as it merely consists of a table look-up procedure. A block diagram of the basic VQ structure is shown in Fig. 12.1.

Compression is obtained in VQ by using a codebook with relatively few codevectors compared to the number of possible image vectors. The resulting bit rate of a VQ scheme is $R = (\log_2 N_c)/n$ bits/pixel. In theory, VQ can achieve performance close to the rate-distortion bound as $n \to \infty$; i.e.,

- for a given average distortion, D, it can achieve compression with the lowest bit rate, and

- for a given average bit rate, R, it can achieve compression with the lowest distortion.

In practice, the large values of n required to approach the rate-distortion bound make codebook storage and searching impractical. Fortunately, reasonable performance can still be achieved with vectors of modest dimension.

To illustrate the effect of vector dimension, consider the VQ encoding of an 8-bit image at a desired bit rate of 1.0 bit/pixel. If the vectors are formed as 2×2 blocks ($n = 4$) of image pixels, the codebook can contain only 16 codevectors ($N_c = 16$), so that $R = (\log_2 16)/4 = 1.0$ bit/pixel. This means that only 16 representative codevectors are available to represent all the 256^4 possible image vectors of size 2×2. If the block size is now increased to 4×4 ($n = 16$), the codebook size for the same bit rate increases to 2^{16} codevectors, which is substantially more than the 16 codevectors available for 2×2 blocks. However, the number of possible image vectors for a 4×4 block is 256^{16}, and the ratio of available codevectors to the total number of possible image vectors decreases.[2] While this situation may seem to yield reduced coding performance, it can be shown that the resulting mean-squared quantization error becomes smaller as the block size is increased.

We now discuss the key elements in the construction of VQ codebook, namely,

- codebook generation, i.e., what codevectors should be included in the codebook, and

- codebook design, i.e., how should the codebook be structured to allow for efficient searching and good performance?

We also discuss several different techniques for forming and encoding image vectors.

12.1   Codebook Generation

12.1.1   Linde-Buzo-Gray (LBG) algorithm

Codebooks are typically generated by using a *training set* of images that are representative of the images to be encoded. This approach has the advantage of not requiring any information about the underlying image statistics. Obviously, to encode any particular image, the optimal codebook would be generated using the image itself as the training set. Such a codebook is called a *local codebook* and usually results in good performance for moderate codebook sizes. This is because most of the image features (such as lines, edges, etc.) that are specific to that particular image are adequately represented by the codevectors. Unfortunately, local codebooks have two disadvantages.

---

[2]For a k-bit image, encoded at a rate of R bits/pixel with block size n, the ratio of number of codevectors to the number of possible image vectors is $2^{n(R-k)}$.

First, a codebook must be generated for every image, which is a computationally intensive task that can hardly be performed in real time. Second, the local codebook must be transmitted to the receiver as overhead information. For example, if the image vectors are formed from 4×4 blocks of pixels ($n = 16$), and each vector component is represented by 8 bits, a codebook of size 2^{10} results in an additional 0.5 bit/pixel of overhead for a 512×512 image.

To overcome the disadvantages associated with a local codebook, a *global codebook* can be generated by using several images as a training set. If the images to be encoded belong to the same class of imagery (in terms of detail, resolution, image features, etc.), a global codebook can result in good performance. An example is the encoding of picture identification cards where all the images are of the head-and-shoulders type with the same resolution. If the images to be encoded differ greatly, the performance of a global codebook may be substantially degraded compared to a local codebook, especially if a small training set has been used. In such cases, the global codebook should be developed using as large and diverse a training set as possible to achieve reasonable average performance. In the VQ results presented later in this section, eight distinctly different images were used as the training set. In some experiments, the image to be encoded was included in the training set and in others it was excluded.

The algorithm generally used to generate VQ codebooks is the Linde-Buzo-Gray (LBG) algorithm [51], which is a generalization of the Lloyd-Max algorithm [10] for scalar quantization discussed in Section 9.1.2. The steps in the LBG algorithm are

1. Start with a set of training vectors, an initial codebook $\hat{\mathbf{X}}_i^{(1)}$, $i = 1, 2, \cdots, N_c$, a distortion measure d, and a fractional distortion change threshold ϵ. Initialize the iteration counter, l, to 1, and initialize the average distortion over all training vectors, $D^{(0)}$, to a very large number.

2. The minimum distortion rule defines a decision region for each codevector $\hat{\mathbf{X}}_i^{(l)}$, so that any training vector enclosed by a particular decision region is mapped to the corresponding $\hat{\mathbf{X}}_i^{(l)}$. Encode the training set by mapping each vector in the training set to its nearest codevector. Compute the average distortion $D^{(l)}$ resulting from the encoding process. If the fractional change in the average distortion from the previous iteration is less than or equal to the threshold, i.e.,

$$\frac{D^{(l-1)} - D^{(l)}}{D^{(l-1)}} \leq \epsilon,$$

then convergence has been achieved and the algorithm terminates. Otherwise, continue to Step 3.

3. Update the codebook by replacing each codevector $\hat{\mathbf{X}}_i^{(l)}$ within a decision region by a new vector $\hat{\mathbf{X}}_i^{(l+1)}$ that minimizes the quantization error within that decision region. For example, for the MSE measure, the minimum distortion codevector is simply the average (centroid) of the training vectors enclosed by that decision region; i.e., each component of the new codevector is found by computing the mean of the corresponding components of the training vectors. Set $l = l + 1$ and go to Step 2. While each iteration results in a nonincreasing distortion, convergence may take many iterations if the threshold ϵ is set too low. As a result, the algorithm is usually terminated after some maximum number of iterations.

As an example of codebook generation, consider using 1×2 pixel blocks of the image LENA as training vectors to construct a codebook with 8 codevectors. Figure 12.2a is a plot of all the pixel pairs of the LENA image (also refer to Fig. 14.2). Use of the LBG algorithm with a MSE distortion criterion and $\epsilon = 0.001$ results in the 8 codevectors shown in Fig. 12.2b. Also shown are the resulting decision regions. By examining the scatter plot of Fig. 12.2a, it is not surprising that all the codevectors lie in the $x_1 = x_2$ direction. Using this codebook to encode LENA results in a bit rate of 1.50 bits/pixel and a MSE of 72.53, where the poor coding performance is due to the small vector dimension and small codebook size. As we shall see, using 4×4 blocks with larger codebooks significantly improves the coding performance.

12.1.2 Codebook initialization

The LBG algorithm only guarantees a locally optimal codebook, and generally numerous local optima will exist. Many of these may yield poor performance, and therefore, choosing an initial codebook is a very important part of the LBG algorithm. Good performance can usually be obtained by providing a good initial codebook [51-53]. In generating an initial codebook, one can start with some simple codebook of the correct size, or one can start with a simple smaller codebook and recursively construct larger ones until the desired size is reached.

- Random Codes [52]: One approach is to use a random initial codebook where the first N_c vectors (or any widely spaced N_c vectors) of the training set are chosen as the initial codebook.

- Splitting [51]: In a splitting procedure, the centroid for the entire training set is found, and this single codeword is then split, i.e., perturbed by a small amount, to form two codewords. The LBG algorithm is applied to get an optimum codebook of size 2. The design continues in this way; i.e., the optimum code of one stage is split to form an initial code for the next stage until N_c codevectors are generated.

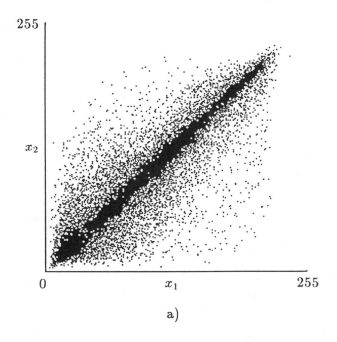

a)

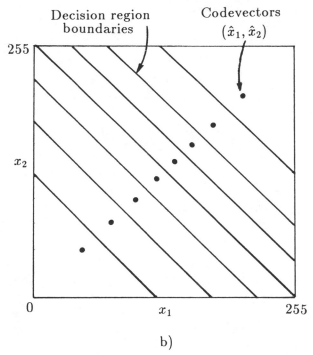

b)

Figure 12.2: Decision regions and codevectors for LENA, 1×2 vectors and $N_c = 8$.

- Pairwise nearest neighbor (PNN) clustering [53]: Starting with N clusters, each containing one training vector, the two closest vectors are merged to create the optimal $(N-1)$ cluster codebook. This process is repeated until the number of clusters equals N_c. The centroids of these clusters are then used as the initial codebook.

12.2 Codebook Design: Tree-Structured Codebooks

In finding the minimum distortion codevector for each image vector, a full search of the codebook can be performed at a computational cost of $\mathcal{O}(nN_c)$. The associated storage cost is nN_c. For large codebooks, the search process becomes computationally intensive. To reduce the search time, a *tree structure* can be imposed on the codebook, where each node has m branches and there are $p = \log_m N_c$ levels to the tree [52,54]. This reduces the computational cost to $\mathcal{O}(nm\log_m N_c)$ since only certain branches of the tree are examined. However, the storage cost increases to $nm(N_c-1)/(m-1)$ since vectors must be stored for every level (including the final level). The codebook is designed by using successive applications of the LBG algorithm at each node for a codebook of size m. An example is shown in Fig. 12.3 for a binary tree ($m = 2$) with $N_c = 8$. In this example, 14 codevectors must be stored (compared to 8 codevectors for a full search), but only 6 codevectors are actually searched in the tree (compared to 8 for a full search).

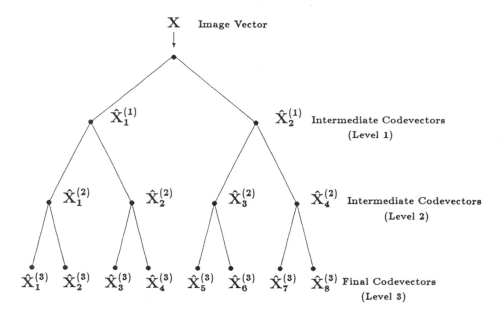

Figure 12.3: Binary VQ tree for $N_c = 8$.

A tree-structured codebook can never perform better than a single-level full-search codebook since a tree structure effectively limits the possible codevectors once a particular branch has been selected.[3] However, by increasing the number of branches at each node, performance can be improved and storage requirements can be reduced. The trade-off is that the number of computations is increased by using more branches. A comparison of the number of computations and the storage required for several different tree structures as well as full-search VQ is given in Table 12.1 for a codebook of size 64.

Technique	Branches per node	Number of nodes	Computations	Storage
Bi-tree	2	6	$\mathcal{O}(12n)$	$126n$
Quad-tree	4	3	$\mathcal{O}(12n)$	$84n$
Oct-tree	8	2	$\mathcal{O}(16n)$	$72n$
Full search	64	1	$\mathcal{O}(64n)$	$64n$

Table 12.1: Comparison of VQ tree structures for $N_c = 64$.

VQ tree structures can also be designed with a nonuniform number of branches at each node. Two such structures are *tapered trees* [55] and *pruned trees* [56]. In tapered trees, the number of branches per node is increased as one moves down the tree, e.g., 2 branches per node at the first level, 3 branches per node at the second level, etc. Improved performance has been reported with such trees as compared to uniform trees [55]. In pruned trees, a large initial tree is pruned by removing codevectors, so that the final tree achieves a given average length with minimum average distortion. The basic idea is to remove those codevectors that do not contribute significantly to reducing the distortion. Pruned trees can be designed for either fixed or variable rate schemes, and reported results for speech signals indicate that pruned tree structures can outperform full-search VQ at a given bit rate [56].

12.3   Codebook Design: Product Codes

As discussed previously, for a constant bit rate $R = (\log_2 N_c)/n$, the performance of VQ improves as the block size n increases. However, since $N_c = 2^{Rn}$, the codebook size (and the encoder complexity) grows exponentially with n. This imposes a severe restriction on the performance of basic VQ.

---

[3]For example, if 1×2 pixel blocks of LENA are used as a training set to develop a tree-structured codebook of size 8 ($m = 2$, $p = 3$), which is then used to encode LENA, the resulting MSE is 75.98 as compared to a MSE of 72.53 for a full-search codebook of size 8.

A solution is to use a codebook with a *product structure*, i.e., a codebook that is formed as the Cartesian product of several smaller codebooks [52]. If a vector can be characterized by certain independent features, e.g., orientation and magnitude, a separate codebook can be developed to encode each feature. The final codeword is the concatenation of all the different encoder outputs. The advantage of a product code can be illustrated by considering an example where two separate codebooks of sizes N_1 and N_2 are used to encode the orientation and the magnitude of a vector, respectively. The effective size (number of codevectors available) of the product codebook is $N_c = N_1 N_2$, since there are N_2 different magnitudes for every orientation. However, the storage and computational complexity is proportional to $N_1 + N_2$ rather than $N_1 N_2$, resulting in a substantial savings. Product codes can also result in more robust codebooks when diverse image types are encoded since the statistical distributions of certain image features are not overly sensitive to the particular input image.

Product codes are suboptimal compared to full-search codebooks of the same effective size, but they can potentially outperform full-search codebooks with the same complexity and bit rate. This is due to the fact that for the same complexity, the effective size of a product codebook is much larger than a full-search codebook, and the product codebook can be used to encode vectors of larger dimension while achieving the same bit rate.

In the following sections we describe several types of product codes, namely, mean/residual VQ (M/RVQ), interpolative/residual VQ (I/RVQ), and gain/shape VQ (G/SVQ). We also describe two other techniques, classified VQ (CVQ) and finite-state VQ (FSVQ), which use several separate, smaller codebooks but are not product codes by the strict definition.

12.4   Mean/Residual VQ (M/RVQ)

One area where product codes can be used to advantage is in the general framework of prediction/residual VQ. In this approach, a prediction is made for the original image based on a limited set of data, and then a residual image is formed by taking the difference between the prediction and the original image. The data used for the prediction are encoded using a scalar quantizer (one-dimensional VQ), and the residual image is encoded using a vector quantizer. This section and the following section describe two types of prediction/residual VQ: mean/residual VQ (M/RVQ) [57] and interpolative/residual VQ (I/RVQ) [58].

The motivation for M/RVQ is that many image vectors (formed from blocks of pixels) exhibit similar variations about different mean levels. By removing the mean from each vector, i.e., the block means, prior to quantization, fewer codevectors are required to represent the residual vectors. In essence, this approach creates a prediction image by replicating each mean value over its corresponding block. This prediction image is then subtracted from the original image to generate the residual.

- The original image is divided into nonoverlapping blocks of size n (typically, $n = 4 \times 4 = 16$) to form the image vectors, and the mean is computed for each block.

- The block means are quantized using a scalar quantizer (typically, 8 bits are used) and transmitted to the receiver. A conventional coding scheme, such as DPCM, can also be used to encode the means to further reduce the bit rate.

- The quantized means are subtracted from their corresponding image vectors to yield residual vectors with approximately zero mean.

- The residual vectors are quantized using VQ, and the indices of the best match residual codevectors are transmitted to the receiver.

- Reconstruction is performed by adding the means to the decoded residual vectors.

12.5 Interpolative/Residual VQ (I/RVQ)

In I/RVQ, a prediction image is formed by subsampling and interpolating the original image, and a residual image is then formed based upon this prediction. This process is very similar to M/RVQ, except that subsampled values are used rather than mean values, and interpolation (usually bilinear) is used rather than replication. The motivation for I/RVQ over M/RVQ is the reduction in blocking artifacts achieved by using a relatively smooth prediction image rather than the replicated block means. I/RVQ results in somewhat better reconstructed image quality than M/RVQ for the same bit rate.

- The original image is subsampled by l (typically, $l = 8$) in each dimension. Each subsampled value is quantized using a scalar quantizer (typically, 8 bits are used) and transmitted to the receiver.

- An approximation (prediction) of the original image is generated at both the receiver and the transmitter by expanding the quantized subsampled values back to the original image size using bilinear interpolation. A residual image is formed by subtracting the subsampled/interpolated image from the original image.

- This residual image is segmented into nonoverlapping blocks of size n (typically, $n = 4 \times 4 = 16$) to form the vectors.

- The residual vectors are quantized using VQ, and the indices of the best match residual codevectors are transmitted to the receiver.

- Reconstruction is performed by adding the decoded residual vectors to the subsampled/interpolated prediction image.

12.6 Gain/Shape VQ (G/SVQ)

In G/SVQ, separate codebooks are used to encode the shape and gain of a vector. The shape is defined as the original image vector normalized by the removal of a gain factor such as the energy or variance of the codevector. Given the gain and shape codebooks, encoding is performed as follows.

- The original image is divided into nonoverlapping blocks of size n (typically, $n = 4 \times 4 = 16$) to form the image vectors.

- A unit energy shape codevector $\mathbf{Y}_j$ is chosen to match the image vector by maximizing the inner product over all codevectors in the shape codebook.

- Given the chosen shape codevector, a scalar gain codeword σ_i is selected so as to minimize the distortion between the image vector X and the reproduction vector $\hat{\mathbf{X}} = \sigma_i \mathbf{Y}_j$. This process is illustrated in Fig. 12.4 for a two-dimensional vector with four possible shape codevectors.

- The indices of the shape codevector and gain codevector are transmitted to the receiver.

- Reconstruction is performed by multiplying the decoded shape and gain codevectors together; i.e., $\hat{\mathbf{X}} = \sigma_i \mathbf{Y}_j$.

12.7 Classified VQ (CVQ)

In CVQ, a number of different codebooks are developed, each designed to encode blocks of pixels that contain a specific type of feature, e.g., a horizontal edge, a vertical edge, completely uniform area, etc. [59]. The codebook used to encode a particular block is determined by a classifier capable of differentiating between the different types of features. The rationale for this approach is that numerous small codebooks, each tuned to a particular class of vectors, can provide comparable image quality with lower search complexity as compared to a single large codebook.

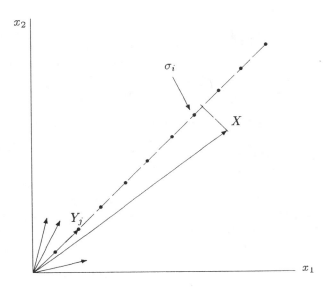

Figure 12.4: Gain and shape vector selection for G/SVQ.

- The original image is divided into nonoverlapping blocks of size n (typically, $n = 4 \times 4 = 16$), and each block is classified into one of M classes using an edge-oriented classifier. Possible classes might include shade blocks (no significant gradient), midrange blocks (moderate gradient, but no definite edge), horizontal edge blocks, vertical edge blocks, 45^0 or 135^0 edge blocks, and mixed blocks (edges with no discernible orientation).

- Each classified block is encoded using the appropriate codebook. The codebooks can be of different sizes, $N_i, i = 1, \ldots, M$, and each codebook can use a different distortion measure in selecting a codevector. The total number of codevectors is $N_c = \sum_{i=1}^{M} N_i$.

- The index of the chosen codevector is sent to the receiver and is used as an entry to a look-up table. Since all possible codevectors are labeled from 1 to N_c, no overhead information is required to indicate the class. It is also possible to separately encode the class (from 1 to M) and the codevector index within a class (from 1 to N_i).

- CVQ can also be used on the residual vectors in a prediction/residual VQ technique.

12.8   Finite-State VQ (FSVQ)

FSVQ is an example of VQ with memory, and it can be modeled as a finite-state machine where each state represents a separate VQ codebook [60]. FSVQ is similar to CVQ in that a collection of relatively small codebooks is used rather than one large codebook. However, in FSVQ, the codebook selection is done on the basis of a next-state function rather than a block classifier. This next-state function is a mapping of the current state (with its associated codebook) and the current output codevector to another state (and associated codebook). The motivation for FSVQ is that adjacent blocks of pixels are often similar, and we can take advantage of this correlation or memory by choosing an appropriate codebook given previous encoding decisions. We note that information theory results imply that VQ with memory can do no better than memoryless VQ, but this is true only for large block sizes, which are difficult to achieve in a practical system. FSVQ results in improved performance with small block sizes since it allows for the use of different quantizers based on past information.

- The original image is divided into nonoverlapping blocks of size n (typically, $n = 4 \times 4 = 16$). These blocks are ordered to form a sequence of image vectors, $\mathbf{X}_i$ ($i = 0, 1, 2, \ldots$).

- Given an initial state s_0 and its associated codebook C_{s_0}, encode the first image vector in the sequence, $\mathbf{X}_0$, by choosing an output codevector, $\hat{\mathbf{X}}_0 \in C_{s_0}$. Transmit the index of this codevector to the receiver.

- Use the next-state function, $f(\cdot)$, to determine the next state, s_1, based on the previous state and output codevector; i.e., $s_1 = f(s_0, \hat{\mathbf{X}}_0)$. Encode the next image vector, $\mathbf{X}_1$, using the codebook associated with state s_1, i.e., $\hat{\mathbf{X}}_1 \in C_{s_1}$, and transmit the index of the chosen codevector.

- Encode the remaining image vectors in the sequence by updating the state for each vector and using the associated codebook; i.e., $s_{n+1} = f(s_n, \hat{\mathbf{X}}_n)$ and $\hat{\mathbf{X}}_{n+1} \in C_{s_{n+1}}$.

- Since the next state is a function of the previous state and the output codevector (not the input image vector), it is possible to track the state changes (and hence the quantizer choices) at the receiver without the use of overhead information. A disadvantage of this approach is that channel errors can propagate, potentially resulting in disasterous reconstruction errors.

12.9 VQ Results

The results of applying M/RVQ and I/RVQ to the two test images are summarized in Table 12.2. For both techniques, the VQ component was performed on 4 × 4 blocks using a tree-structured codebook. Since a tree structure was used, the techniques are denoted as mean/residual tree-structured VQ (M/RTVQ) and interpolative/residual tree-structured VQ (I/RTVQ). The codebook had 8 ($= 2^3$) branches at each node (oct-tree) and a total of 5 levels for a final size of 2^{15} codevectors. The incremental bit rate for each level was 3/16 bit/pixel. The training set consisted of eight 512 × 512 images representing different classes of imagery, and results are shown for both inclusion and exclusion of the encoded image in the training set.

For M/RTVQ, the mean of each block was quantized to 8 bits, which results in an initial bit rate of $8/16 = 0.5$ bit/pixel and a final bit rate of $0.5 + \left(\frac{3}{16} \times 5\right) = 1.438$ bits/pixel. For I/RTVQ, the original image was subsampled by 8 in each direction, and each subsampled pixel was transmitted using 8 bits. This results in an initial bit rate of $8/64 = 0.125$ bit/pixel and a final bit rate of $0.125 + \left(\frac{3}{16} \times 5\right) = 1.063$ bits/pixel.

Reconstructed and error images using I/RTVQ on LENA are shown in Figs. 12.5 - 12.10, corresponding to bit rates of 0.13, 0.31, 0.50, 0.69, 0.87, and 1.06 bits/pixel, respectively. LENA was excluded from the training set for these images. The reconstructed image at 0.13 bit/pixel is the subsampled/interpolated image with no codevectors added to it; that is, it is the prediction image. The corresponding error image at 0.13 bit/pixel is the residual image that is encoded using VQ (the residual has been scaled by a factor of two and biased by 127 in Fig. 12.5).

A magnified section of the residual (biased by 127, but with no scaling) is shown at the top of Fig. 12.11. To illustrate typical codevectors used to encode the residual image, the first two levels of the codebook, containing 8 and 64 codevectors, respectively, are shown in Fig. 12.12. The bottom of Fig. 12.11 shows the encoded residual obtained using codevectors selected from level 2 of the codebook. By adding this encoded residual to the prediction image, we obtain the reconstructed image at the bottom of Fig. 12.13. In the enlarged image at 0.50 bit/pixel, blocking artifacts are apparent, and it is obvious that the use of only 64 different codevectors is not sufficient to adequately represent all possible 4 × 4 blocks.

Technique	Bit rate bits/pixel	LENA		BOOTS	
		RMSE (0-255)	SNR (dB)	RMSE (0-255)	SNR (dB)
M/RTVQ (Include)					
Level 0	0.50	11.52	26.90	19.59	22.29
Level 1	0.69	8.62	29.42	14.70	24.79
Level 2	0.87	6.60	31.74	11.46	26.95
Level 3	1.06	5.25	33.72	9.29	28.77
Level 4	1.25	4.27	35.51	7.40	30.75
Level 5	1.44	3.27	37.85	4.86	34.39
M/RTVQ (Exclude)					
Level 0	0.50	11.52	26.90	19.59	22.29
Level 1	0.69	8.75	29.29	14.72	24.77
Level 2	0.87	6.64	31.68	11.61	26.83
Level 3	1.06	5.37	33.53	9.61	28.47
Level 4	1.25	4.63	34.82	8.45	29.59
Level 5	1.44	4.24	35.58	7.85	30.24
I/RTVQ (Include)					
Level 0	0.13	16.21	23.94	27.62	19.31
Level 1	0.31	10.68	27.56	18.18	22.94
Level 2	0.50	8.05	30.02	14.09	25.15
Level 3	0.69	6.41	31.99	11.39	27.00
Level 4	0.87	5.19	33.83	9.06	28.99
Level 5	1.06	3.96	36.18	5.99	32.58
I/RTVQ (Exclude)					
Level 0	0.13	16.21	23.94	27.62	19.31
Level 1	0.31	10.75	27.50	18.09	22.98
Level 2	0.50	8.11	29.95	14.14	25.12
Level 3	0.69	6.53	31.83	11.69	26.78
Level 4	0.87	5.65	33.09	10.25	27.92
Level 5	1.06	5.23	33.77	9.57	28.52

Table 12.2: VQ results.

12.10 Implementation Issues and Complexity of M/RTVQ and I/RTVQ Algorithms

As with the DCT and AMBTC algorithms, the M/RTVQ and I/RTVQ algorithms are also amenable to parallel processing, but again we will assume sequential processing. Two factors contribute to the complexity of the these algorithms. One is forming the residual image, and the other is the VQ encoding. The major complexity is the VQ encoding process, and this aspect is discussed first.

For the tree-structured VQ encoding, it is assumed that the codebook of size N_c has p levels and m branches at each node such that $p = \log_m N_c$. It is further assumed that those quantities in the distortion measure that are independent of the input vector have been precomputed and stored. For example, for a squared error distortion measure and a given input vector $\mathbf{X}$ and codevector $\hat{\mathbf{X}}$, the distortion is proportional to

$$\sum_{i=1}^{n}(x_i - \hat{x}_i)^2 = \sum_{i=1}^{n} x_i{}^2 - 2\sum_{i=1}^{n} x_i\hat{x}_i + \sum_{i=1}^{n} \hat{x}_i^2. \qquad (12.3)$$

The first term in Eq. (12.3) is constant for a given input vector and can be disregarded, while the last term is dependent only on the codevector and can be computed prior to encoding. Therefore, computation of the distortion measure for each codevector requires only one multiplication per pixel to form the product in the second term (the factor of 2 can be included in the codevector) and one addition per pixel to sum these products and add in the last term. Since m possible codevectors are searched at each level and there are p levels, a total of pm additions and pm multiplications per pixel are required to reach the final level of the codebook. For a vector of size n, the number of comparisons per pixel at each level is $(m-1)/n$ for a total of $p(m-1)/n$ comparisons to reach the final level. Thus, the number of operations at the final level for the VQ encoding with $m = 8$ and $p = 5$ is

- 40 multiplications,

- 40 additions, and

- 2.19 comparisons

per pixel.

For M/RTVQ, the formation of the residual image requires 4×4 block means to be computed and subtracted from the original image at a cost of approximately 2 additions per pixel. (The one multiplication required in computing the block mean may be performed by logical shifts and will be disregarded.) For I/RTVQ, the formation of residual image requires bilinear interpolation to expand the subsampled image by a factor of 8 in each direction. An efficient implementation can perform this step using 3 multiplications and 4 additions per pixel. An extra addition (subtraction) per pixel is also required to form the actual residual image. The total number of operations for the residual formation and VQ encoding is then

- 40 (for M/RTVQ) or 43 (for I/RTVQ) multiplications,

- 42 (for M/RTVQ) or 45 (for I/RTVQ) additions, and

- 2.19 comparisons

per pixel. The decoder complexity is similar to the encoder in forming the residual image, but the actual VQ decoding is a simple table look-up.

The number of memory locations required to store a tree-structured codebook is given by

$$\text{Memory} = n(N_c - 1)\frac{m}{m - 1}, \tag{12.4}$$

where one storage location is assumed for each codevector component. For $m = 8$, $p = 5$, and $n = 16$ (4×4 blocks), the required storage is 599,168 storage locations (37,448 codevectors). Because of the tree structure, only 40 codevectors are actually searched to reach the final level. In comparison, a full-search codebook of the same final size requires 524,288 storage locations (32,768 codevectors), but all codevectors are searched. Working memory requirements are to the extent needed to store the lines of the input pixels and form the blocks.

In VQ techniques such as M/RTVQ and I/RTVQ, the effect of channel errors is confined to a single VQ block. For VQ techniques with memory such as FSVQ, errors can propagate because future states may be misclassified.

Figure 12.5: I/RTVQ at 0.13 bit/pixel.

Figure 12.6: I/RTVQ at 0.31 bit/pixel.

Figure 12.7: I/RTVQ at 0.50 bit/pixel.

Figure 12.8: I/RTVQ at 0.69 bit/pixel.

Figure 12.9: I/RTVQ at 0.87 bit/pixel.

Figure 12.10: I/RTVQ at 1.06 bits/pixel.

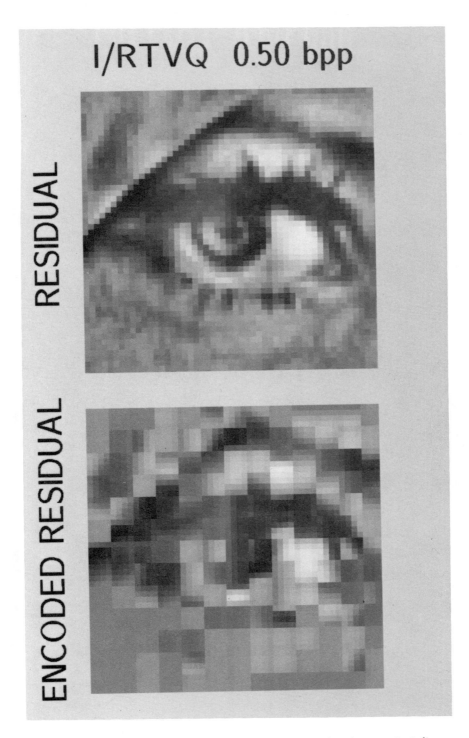

Figure 12.11: Residual image for I/RTVQ: original (top), encoded (bottom).

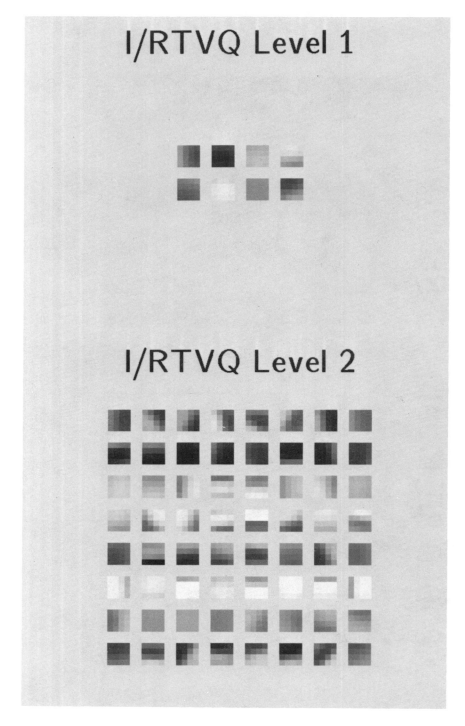

Figure 12.12: Residual codebook for I/RTVQ: level 1 (top), level 2 (bottom).

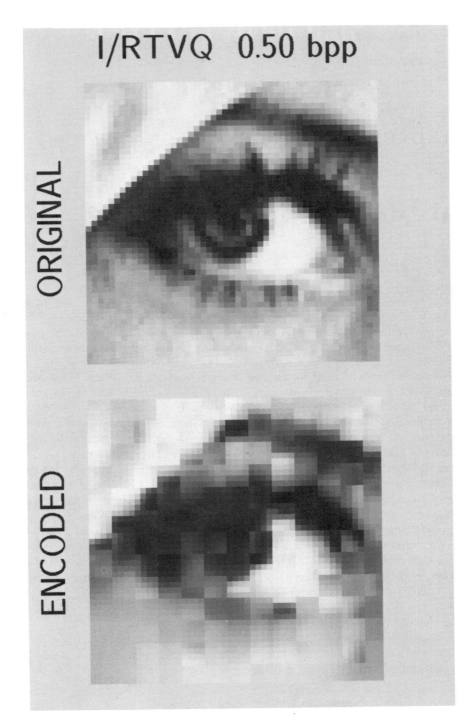

Figure 12.13: Original (top), I/RTVQ at 0.50 bit/pixel (bottom) (magnified).

Chapter 13

Subband Coding

In *subband coding* (SBC), an image is first filtered to create a set of images, each of which contains a limited range of spatial frequencies. These images are called the *subbands*. Since each subband has a reduced bandwidth compared to the original full-band image, they may be downsampled. This process of filtering and subsampling is termed the *analysis stage*. The subbands are then encoded using one or more coders. Different bit rates or even different coding techniques can be used for each subband, thus taking advantage of the properties of the subband and/or allowing for the coding errors to be distributed across the subbands in a visually optimal manner. Reconstruction is achieved by upsampling the decoded subbands, applying appropriate filters, and adding the reconstructed subbands together. This is termed the *synthesis stage*. Note that the formation of subbands does not create any compression in itself (since the same total number of samples is required to represent the subbands as is required for the original image). The motivation for this approach is that the subbands can be encoded more efficiently than the original image. A block diagram for a basic 1-D, two-band system is shown in Fig. 13.1, where the downsampling is by a factor of two. In this diagram, the analysis filters, $h_1(n)$ and $h_2(n)$, are lowpass and highpass, respectively, and $g_1(n)$ and $g_2(n)$ are the corresponding synthesis filters.

The key elements in a SBC system are

- the analysis and synthesis filtering banks and

- the coding technique(s) applied to the subbands.

The analysis and synthesis filtering banks are first described for 1-D signals and then extended to 2-D signals.

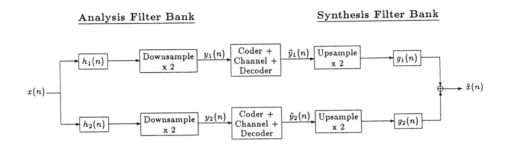

Figure 13.1: 1-D, two-band SBC block diagram.

13.1 Analysis/Synthesis Filtering for 1-D Signals

In order to decompose a full-band, 1-D signal into two subbands, the analysis filter bank would ideally consist of a lowpass and a highpass filter set with frequency responses that are nonoverlapping, but contiguous, and have unity gain over their bandwidths. However, ideal filters are unrealizable in practice, and it is necessary to use filters with overlapping responses in order to prevent frequency gaps in signals represented by the subbands. The problem with overlapping filters is that aliasing is introduced when the subbands are downsampled.

To overcome this problem, analysis and synthesis filtering is typically done using *quadrature mirror filters* (QMFs), which allow for an alias-free reconstruction in the absence of coding errors [61]. The name quadrature mirror filter arises from the fact that the filters exhibit mirror symmetry about $\pi/2$ radians (which is one-quarter of the normalized sampling frequency). An idealized lowpass and highpass QMF pair is illustrated in Fig. 13.2. The philosophy of QMFs is to allow aliasing to be introduced by using overlapping filters for the analysis bank and then design the synthesis filters in such a way that any aliasing is exactly cancelled out in the reconstruction process. Of course, these filters are also designed so that overall amplitude and phase distortion are minimized or eliminated.

The derivation of the required frequency response for QMFs is relatively straightforward. Referring to Fig. 13.1, the output signals from the analysis

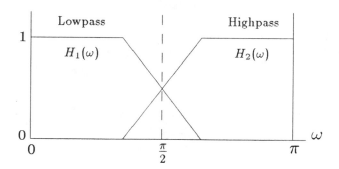

Figure 13.2: 1-D idealized QMF pair.

bank after downsampling by a factor of two are

$$Y_1(z) = \frac{1}{2}[H_1(z^{\frac{1}{2}}) \cdot X(z^{\frac{1}{2}}) + H_1(-z^{\frac{1}{2}}) \cdot X(-z^{\frac{1}{2}})], \qquad (13.1)$$

$$Y_2(z) = \frac{1}{2}[H_2(z^{\frac{1}{2}}) \cdot X(z^{\frac{1}{2}}) + H_2(-z^{\frac{1}{2}}) \cdot X(-z^{\frac{1}{2}})], \qquad (13.2)$$

where z-transforms have been used for the spectra.[1] The reconstructed signal is found by summing the outputs from the synthesis bank after up-sampling:

$$\hat{X}(z) = \hat{Y}_1(z^2) \cdot G_1(z) + \hat{Y}_2(z^2) \cdot G_2(z). \qquad (13.3)$$

Ignoring any coding effects, i.e., set $\hat{Y}_i(z) = Y_i(z)$ for $i = 1, 2$, Eq. (13.3) is equivalent to

$$\hat{X}(z) = \frac{1}{2}[H_1(z) \cdot G_1(z) + H_2(z) \cdot G_2(z)] \cdot X(z)$$

$$+ \frac{1}{2}[H_1(-z) \cdot G_1(z) + H_2(-z) \cdot G_2(z)] \cdot X(-z). \qquad (13.4)$$

---

[1] The z-transform $X(z)$ of a sequence $x(n)$ is given by

$$X(z) = \sum_{n=-\infty}^{\infty} x(n) z^{-n},$$

where z is a complex variable. If $z = e^{j\omega}$, then the z-transform of the sequence is equivalent to its Fourier transform.

The second term represents the aliased component, which we desire to be zero. If we use symmetric (linear phase) FIR filters and let

$$H_2(z) = H_1(-z) \quad \Rightarrow \quad h_2(n) = (-1)^n h_1(n), \tag{13.5}$$

$$G_1(z) = 2H_1(z) \quad \Rightarrow \quad g_1(n) = 2h_1(n), \tag{13.6}$$

$$G_2(z) = -2H_2(z) \quad \Rightarrow \quad g_2(n) = -2(-1)^n h_1(n), \tag{13.7}$$

then the aliased term becomes zero and the reconstructed signal is given by

$$\hat{X}(z) = [H_1^2(z) - H_2^2(z)] \cdot X(z). \tag{13.8}$$

The overall transfer function for the system is thus

$$T(z) = H_1^2(z) - H_2^2(z). \tag{13.9}$$

Since both $H_1(z)$ and $H_2(z)$ have linear phase, the system introduces no phase distortion. The remaining problem is to eliminate amplitude distortion by making $T(z)$ equal to 1 for every z. This will allow for *perfect reconstruction*; i.e., $\hat{x}(n) = x(n)$. The only linear phase FIR filter capable of achieving this goal has exactly two taps (coefficients) [62]. Unfortunately, the frequency separation of the two-tap lowpass and highpass filters is quite poor, which reduces the subsequent coding efficiency. In practice, some amplitude distortion must be tolerated, and the filters are designed using various optimization techniques employing constraints on passband ripple, stopband rejection, and transition region bandwidth. In general, larger filters, i.e., those with more taps, yield better coding performance at the expense of an increased computational load.

An important aspect of the system just described is that the filters must have an *even* number of taps. This can be seen by examining $T(z)$ in the frequency domain. It can be shown [61] that using linear phase FIR analysis and synthesis filters of length N results in

$$T(e^{j\omega}) = \left[|H_1(e^{j\omega})|^2 - (-1)^{(N-1)} |H_2(e^{j\omega})|^2 \right] e^{-j\omega(N-1)}. \tag{13.10}$$

For odd N, the frequency response at $\omega = \pi/2$ is zero, implying severe amplitude distortion. It is possible to modify the system shown in Fig. 13.1 by introducing one-pixel delays to allow for the use of odd-tap filters [63]. It has been reported that odd-tap filters can be of shorter length than even-tap filters while still maintaining good performance [64].

There are other possible approaches to subband filter design that yield substantially different filter characteristics. One approach results in a class of filters known as conjugate quadrature filters (CQFs) [65]. These analysis/synthesis filters have nonsymmetrical coefficients and nonlinear phase, but the resulting overall system has linear phase and perfect reconstruction capability. Another approach is a class of symmetric short-kernel analysis/synthesis filters that also have perfect reconstruction capability [66]. Filters designed using these approaches may prove advantageous in some situations, but they, as well as the more typical QMFs, should be evaluated carefully to determine their suitability for the given application.

13.2   Extension to 2-D Signals

Extending the results in the previous section to 2-D signals is relatively straightforward due to the fact that the required 2-D QMFs can be designed as separable filters [67]. Therefore, the 1-D filters can be applied first in one dimension and then in the other dimension to generate the subbands. This is the approach typically used in subband coding of images. Note that subsampling can be done after filtering in the first dimension to reduce the number of operations required for filtering in the other dimension. The process is shown in Fig. 13.3 for the analysis bank and in Fig. 13.4 for the synthesis bank, where a total of four subbands have been generated. The subbands are lowpass/lowpass, lowpass/highpass, highpass/lowpass, and highpass/highpass in the horizontal and vertical directions, respectively. The approximate frequency range of each subband is illustrated in Fig. 13.5, where 11 designates the lowpass/lowpass subband, 12 designates the lowpass/highpass subband, etc. If more than four subbands are desired, then the QMF structure can be applied repeatedly to one or more subbands. For example, each of the four subbands may be split again to generate 16 subbands, or often only the lowpass/lowpass subband is split to generate 7 subbands (of differing dimensions).

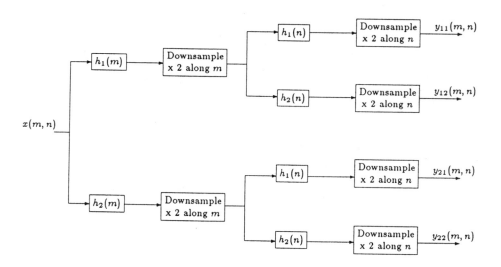

Figure 13.3: 2-D, four-band analysis bank.

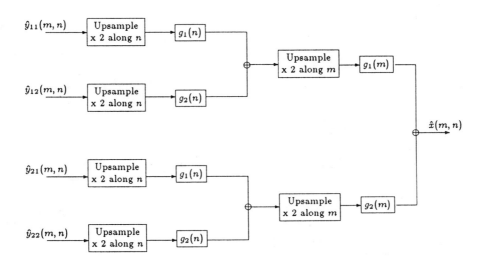

Figure 13.4: 2-D, four-band synthesis bank.

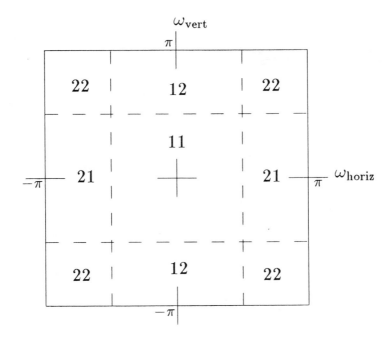

Figure 13.5: Approximate frequency ranges for a four-band split.

Illustrated in Figs. 13.6 and 13.7 are the subbands from 4-band and 16-band splits of LENA, respectively. These images were generated using a 32-tap QMF, denoted 32-D in [62]. Except for the lowest frequency subbands (labeled 11 in Fig. 13.6 and 11-11 in Fig. 13.7), all images have been scaled by a factor of 8 and biased by 128 to accentuate the structure in the subbands.

Tables 13.1 and 13.2 list the mean and variance of each subband (with no bias or scaling) for the 4-band and 16-band splits of LENA. The subbands have been ordered by using a zigzag scan (similar to the way DCT coefficients are ordered), which results in the variances being ranked approximately in terms of decreasing value. It is interesting to note that for any particular subband decomposition, the sum of the subband variances is equal to the variance of the image (or subband) that was split. For example, the sum of the variances of the four subbands formed from the original image (11,21,12, and 22 in Table 13.1) is roughly equal to the variance of the original. This is a demonstration of *error variance preservation*; that is, any error variance introduced in the subbands (through quantization or deletion of subbands, for example) is preserved in the reconstructed image. It can be shown that this will be true for QMFs if and only if $T(z)$ in Eq. (13.9) is equal to 1 for every z [68]. Also note that the means of the lowest frequency subbands, e.g., 11 and 11-11, are equal to the mean of the original image, while the remaining subbands have essentially zero mean.

Figure 13.6: Four-band split of LENA.

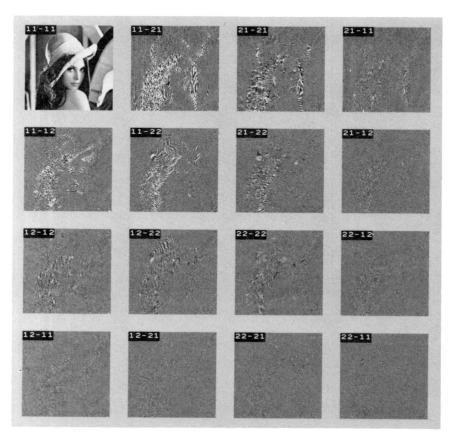

Figure 13.7: 16-band split of LENA.

Subband	Mean	Variance
11	123.60	2282.03
12	0.01	4.06
21	0.01	10.30
22	0.00	2.23
Sum	123.62	2298.62
Original	123.61	2298.65

Table 13.1: Means and variances for a four-band split of LENA.

Subband	Mean	Variance
11-11	123.60	2230.78
11-12	0.01	11.05
11-21	0.01	32.02
21-21	-0.02	5.41
11-22	0.01	8.12
12-12	0.01	1.37
12-11	0.01	0.65
12-22	-0.02	1.54
21-22	0.00	2.41
21-11	0.02	1.61
21-12	0.01	0.87
22-22	-0.01	0.86
12-21	0.00	0.49
22-21	0.00	0.47
22-12	0.00	0.52
22-11	0.00	0.37
Sum	123.63	2298.40
Original	123.61	2298.65

Table 13.2: Means and variances for a 16-band split of LENA.

13.3   Subband Coding Techniques

Subband coding is motivated by the idea that the subbands can be coded more efficiently than the entire full band image. The following techniques have been proposed for coding subband images.

13.3.1   DPCM encoding

Each subband is encoded using DPCM [67]. This is a good technique for a small number of subbands since each subband will still have significant pixel-to-pixel correlation.

13.3.2   DPCM/PCM encoding

DPCM encoding is performed only on the lowest subband where pixel-to-pixel correlation is high, and straight quantization (PCM encoding) is performed on all other subbands where correlation is low [69]. Each subband uses a different quantizer to allocate noise appropriately. This technique is good for a large number of subbands since the higher-order subbands will have power spectral densities that are nearly white; that is, the subbands have very little spatial correlation.

13.3.3   VQ encoding

Vectors can be formed from the subbands in two ways. One approach is to segment each subband into blocks (typically, 4×4 blocks). The vectors are thus formed *within* the subbands. One or more codebooks are then designed, each tailored to a specific subband or subbands. The second approach is to concatenate a pixel from the same spatial location in each subband (typically, 16 subbands) [70]. Here, the vectors are formed *across* subbands. A single codebook is designed to achieve the appropriate image quality and bit rate. In either approach, a training set of suitable subband images is used to generate the VQ codebook(s).

13.4 Relationship Between Subband Coding and Transform Coding

In the subband coding techniques we have described, an image is decomposed into a set of bandpass filtered subimages using FIR analysis filters such as QMFs. Intuitively, this process seems to be related to the basis function decomposition that occurs in block transform coding. Both approaches provide a localized frequency representation of the original image. In fact, there is a well-defined correspondence between the subband and transform representations of a signal [71]. The difference between the two approaches lies primarily in the manner in which the output data are organized.

This difference can be best explained pictorially. Consider a transform (such as the DFT or DCT) that is applied to 2×2 nonoverlapping blocks of an image. Referring to Fig. 13.8a, we see that each transformed block contains four transform coefficients, labeled a (the lowest frequency) to d (the highest frequency). Now consider decomposing the same image by using 2×2 analysis filters and decimating by a factor of two in each direction. It can be shown that by designing an *appropriate* set of analysis filters, a subband representation can be found that is entirely equivalent to the transform representation. Referring to Fig. 13.8b, the lowpass/lowpass subband image merely corresponds to a grouping of the lowest frequency coefficients, one from each transformed block. The other transform coefficients are similarly grouped to form the remaining subband images. Since each transform block is 2×2, this reordering results in a four-band split of the original image. This process can also be viewed from the other direction, where the subband images are reordered to form the transform coefficient blocks. The choice of one representation or the other is determined primarily by the application.

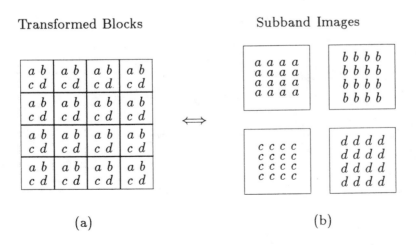

(a)　　　　　　　　　　　　(b)

Figure 13.8: Equivalence between transform and subband representations.

In general, the exact relationship between the transform kernel and the subband analysis and synthesis filters is more complex than this simple example suggests. This is because a subband filter with a length larger than the decimation factor, e.g., an 8-tap filter and decimation by two at each stage, corresponds to a *lapped orthogonal transform* (LOT), where the transform is applied to overlapping blocks of pixels [71]. Lapped transforms are used to reduce the blocking artifacts that can occur with disjoint block transforms. Since the subband filter lengths are typically much greater than the decimation factor, blocking is generally not a problem in subband coding.

The observation that there is a direct relationship between subband coding and transform coding can provide additional insights. For example, in transform coding, a common technique is to use zonal coding, where only certain prespecified coefficients are retained. In subband coding, the analogous approach is to retain only certain prespecified subbands. Similarly, the application of VQ *across* the subbands is identical to applying VQ to individual blocks of transformed data. Also, the error variance preservation property of QMFs described previously is equivalent to the distance-preserving property of orthogonal transforms. That is, the MSE between the original image and the reconstructed image is equal to the MSE introduced in the subbands or the transform coefficients by any quantization or coding process.

13.5   SBC Results

The results of applying subband coding with VQ across the subbands are summarized in Table 13.3 for the two test images. The subbands were generated using 32-tap (designated 32-D in [62]) analysis and synthesis filters. A tree-structured codebook (oct-tree) of size 2^{15} was used on vectors formed across 16 subbands. The training set for the VQ codebook consisted of the

Technique	Bit rate bits/pixel	LENA		BOOTS	
		RMSE (0-255)	SNR (dB)	RMSE (0-255)	SNR (dB)
SBC/VQ					
Level 2	0.38	7.46	30.68	12.71	26.05
Level 3	0.56	5.91	32.71	10.66	27.58
Level 4	0.75	5.10	33.98	9.39	28.68
Level 5	0.94	4.70	34.69	8.72	29.32

Table 13.3: SBC results.

subbands of eight 512×512 images, and both test images were excluded from the training set.

Reconstructed and error images using SBC/VQ on LENA are shown in Figs. 13.9 - 13.12 for bit rates of 0.38, 0.56, 0.75, and 0.94 bit/pixel, respectively. A magnified section of LENA reconstructed at 0.56 bit/pixel is shown in Fig. 13.13, along with a magnified section of the original image for comparison. From this figure, it can be seen that performing VQ across the subbands results in substantially less blocking artifacts than performing VQ directly on blocks of image data.

13.6 Implementation Issues and Complexity of SBC/VQ Algorithm

In this section, only the subband filtering portion of the algorithm is discussed. Refer to the chapter on VQ for a discussion of its corresponding complexity. It is also noted that the subband filtering process could be implemented in a highly parallel manner given enough hardware. In this discussion, it is assumed that the system is implemented in a tree structure as shown in Figs. 13.3 and 13.4, with sequential processing of the branches.

At each stage of the subband analysis bank, the image is filtered along one dimension by a set of lowpass and highpass filters and is decimated by a factor of two along that dimension as shown in Fig. 13.3. To generate each lowpass or highpass filtered point remaining after decimation, 32 multiplications and 31 additions are required for the 32-tap filter used. Owing to symmetries between the lowpass and highpass filters, i.e., $h(n)$ and $(-1)^n h(n)$, the same multiplications can be used for both filters [67]. Therefore, to produce a pair of lowpass and highpass filtered points at each stage requires 32 multiplications and 62 additions.[2] Since a 16-band split is performed, there are four stages with $N(N/2)$ filtered pairs of points in the first stage, $2(N/2)(N/2)$ in the second, $4(N/2)(N/4)$ in the third, and $8(N/4)(N/4)$ in the fourth, assuming an $N \times N$ original image. It can be seen that each stage has $N^2/2$ pairs of filtered points, resulting in a total of $64N^2$ multiplications and $124N^2$ additions. Referenced to the original image, this is

- 64 multiplications and

- 124 additions

per pixel to create the entire 16 bands using the 32-tap filter.

---

[2]Since the filters themselves are symmetric, it is possible to further reduce the number of multiplications by a factor of two at the expense of increased complexity and storage.

At each stage of the synthesis bank, the subbands are interpolated by a factor of two and filtered along one of the dimensions. Each output point from a given stage requires 16 multiplications (since every other point is zero from the interpolation) and 15 additions. It can be shown that each stage produces $2N^2$ output points, resulting in $32N^2$ multiplications and $30N^2$ additions per stage. Each stage also requires N^2 extra additions to add the subbands together. The total number is then $128N^2$ multiplications and $124N^2$ additions per synthesized image. Referenced to the original image, this is

- 128 multiplications and

- 124 additions

per pixel. It is obvious from the number of multiplications and additions that the use of a 32-tap filter results in a large computational load in both the analysis and synthesis stages. In a real time application, it would be necessary to use a much smaller filter length to achieve the necessary throughput.

Permanent memory required for this scheme is quite high since the codevectors for the VQ component must be stored. However, the subband filtering portion requires only that the filter coefficients be stored. Working memory can also be significant depending on the implementation. In general, it is necessary to provide storage for the intermediate images and the final subband images at the encoder and for the intermediate reconstructed images at the decoder.

For many SBC schemes, the effect of a channel error is typically confined to a single subband, and the overall reconstruction quality may not be greatly affected, particularly if the error occurs in one of the higher frequency bands. For the SBC/VQ technique described in this chapter, the VQ is performed across the subbands, and a channel error affects the same spatial location in all of the subbands. This increases the effects of the error to some extent, but the error will still be limited to a relatively small region of the reconstructed image.

Figure 13.9: SBC/VQ at 0.38 bit/pixel.

Figure 13.10: SBC/VQ at 0.56 bit/pixel.

Figure 13.11: SBC/VQ at 0.75 bit/pixel.

Figure 13.12: SBC/VQ at 0.94 bit/pixel.

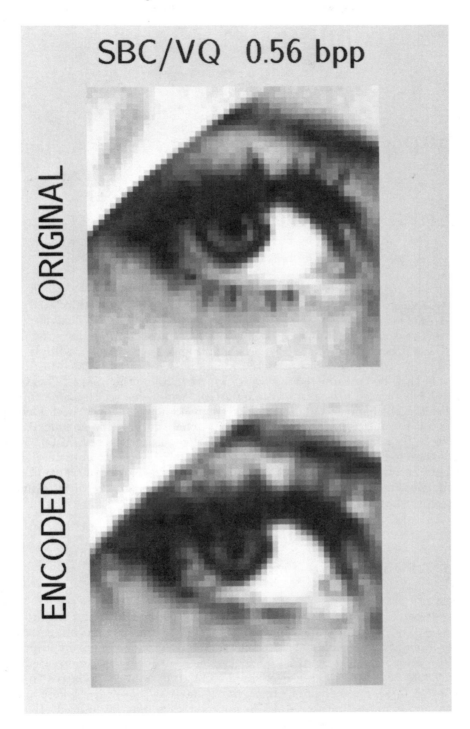

Figure 13.13: Original (top), SBC/VQ at 0.56 bit/pixel (bottom) (magnified).

Chapter 14

Hierarchical Coding

In *hierarchical coding*, image data are encoded in such a way that it is possible to access a given image at different quality levels or resolutions. For example, in searching an image database, hierarchical coding allows the user to initially access a low-quality version of an image (at a correspondingly low bit rate) in order to determine if the image is the desired one. Additional data can then be transmitted in stages to further refine the image. This type of scheme is termed *progressive transmission*. As another example, an image database might be used to support a number of output devices, each having a different resolution. A hierarchical coding scheme allows for each device to efficiently access a version of the image with the appropriate resolution. This is an example of a *multiuse environment*. We now discuss in more detail the concepts and desired characteristics of schemes for progressive transmission and multiuse environments. This is followed by descriptions of various image hierarchies that are useful for such applications.

14.1 Progressive Transmission

In progressive transmission (PT), partial image information is transmitted in stages, and at each stage, an approximation to the original image is reconstructed at the receiver. The reconstructed images progressively improve as more information is received. Progressive transmission is motivated by the need to transmit images over low-bandwidth channels (relative to the amount of data), e.g., telephone lines, particularly in those cases where quick recognition is important or total transmission time may be limited. Examples of this scenario include telebrowsing, where a remote image database is searched for a particular image or images, and photojournalism or military applications, where a user may have only limited access to communication channels. Of course, conventional compression algorithms will decrease the transmission time, but they generally require the majority of the image to be reconstructed to achieve recognition and permit only a single reconstructed image of fixed quality.

An important aspect of PT is that the transmission can be stopped if an intermediate version of the image is satisfactory or if the image is found to be of no interest. This reduction in transmitted data due to user termination is called *effective compression*. In addition to providing possible effective compression, many PT schemes incorporate conventional compression techniques such as variable-length coding or DPCM to reduce the overall bit rate. The techniques used in PT can be either lossy or lossless at the final stage of transmission. Even those techniques that are inherently lossy can be made lossless by additionally transmitting a lossless residual error image. (Refer to Chapter 8: Lossy Plus Lossless Residual Encoding for more details.)

There are several characteristics that are desirable in a PT scheme. They include

- A low bit rate for the early approximations where the decision is made to retain or reject the image. This allows for large effective compression.

- Making maximum use of all previously transmitted data so that the additional information required for the next stage is kept to a minimum.

- The capability to fully transmit an image at a low total bit rate and with excellent (perhaps lossless) image quality.

- Encoding/decoding algorithms that are relatively fast and are amenable to hardware implementations.

14.2 Multiuse Environments

In a multiuse environment, compressed image data are made available to a number of display or transmission devices with differing resolution or quality requirements, e.g., an HDTV video monitor, a high-resolution hardcopy output scanner, a low-resolution transmitter for telephone lines, etc. The desired characteristics of a multiuse scheme are similar to those of PT, and they include

- Efficient storage of the image data, and efficient access to the different resolutions or quality levels.

- Making maximum use of lower resolution data so that the additional information required to reconstruct the next higher level image is kept to a minimum.

- The capability to recover the full-resolution original image at a low total bit rate and with excellent (perhaps lossless) image quality.

- Encoding/decoding algorithms that are relatively fast and are amenable to hardware implementations. In particular, efficient decoding algorithms are desired since a multiuse environment is typically centered around a database, implying write once/read many times.

14.3   Image Hierarchies

The common aspect of PT and multiuse environments is the need for *image hierarchies*, i.e., a way to organize the image data in order of importance. Typically, we speak of the various levels of the hierarchy, where each level corresponds to a reconstructed image at a particular resolution or level of quality. Hierarchies find use in other areas of image processing besides image compression, and they can be based on a variety of image attributes. For our purposes, it is convenient to classify them into fixed-resolution hierarchies or variable-resolution hierarchies.

In fixed-resolution hierarchies, the reconstructed image is inherently the same size as the original image, and the value at any particular pixel location is refined as one moves from level to level. This type of hierarchy is used primarily for progressive transmission applications since it is poorly suited to multiuse environments where the devices require different spatial resolutions.

In variable-resolution hierarchies, the images corresponding to the levels of the hierarchy vary in spatial resolution. This approach naturally results in a *pyramid structure*, where the base of the pyramid represents the full-resolution image, i.e., the original image, and as one moves up the pyramid, the images decrease in spatial resolution and size. For example, if the levels of the hierarchy are formed by repeatedly averaging over 2×2 blocks, then the pyramid representation would appear as in Fig. 14.1. The connections between pixels at the various levels are explicitly shown in this figure, and it is easy to see that these connections define an equivalent tree structure. Each node of the tree (which corresponds to a pixel value) has four branches whose nodes indicate the four pixels that were averaged. Obviously, the variable-resolution hierarchy is particularly suited to a multiuse environment supporting devices of varying resolutions as well as being useful for progressive transmission. For display purposes in a PT scheme, it may be desirable to interpolate or replicate the reduced size images to a larger size for improved recognizability.

An important distinction between the two classes is in the *incremental bit rate*, i.e., the number of bits required to move from one level of the hierarchy to the next (normalized to the number of pixels in the original image).

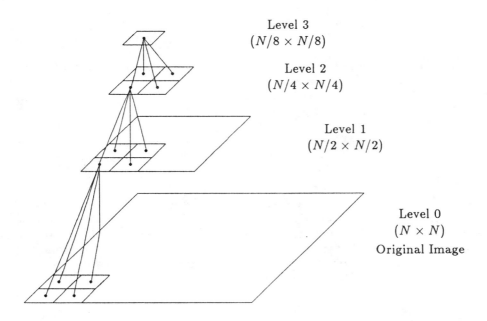

Figure 14.1: 2×2 subsampling pyramid/tree structure.

In the fixed-resolution techniques, the incremental bit rate is held more or less constant as one moves through the levels. While a constant incremental increase in the number of transmitted bits does not necessarily correspond to constant incremental improvements in image quality, it does allow the reconstructed image to be refined at fixed time intervals. In comparison, the incremental bit rate for the variable-resolution techniques grows exponentially as one moves to higher resolution levels. For example, increasing the image dimensions by a factor of two between each level results in an incremental bit rate that quadruples from one level to the next. Thus, it takes longer to transmit and reconstruct as the progression proceeds, which may be a problem in some systems.

14.4   Fixed-Resolution Hierarchies

14.4.1   Bit planes

As described in Chapter 6, a k-bit image can be represented by k bit planes, each of the same dimension as the original image. Progressive transmission can be easily achieved by transmitting the bit planes in a sequence, starting with the most significant bit plane and ending with the least significant bit plane. The image reconstructed from the most significant bit plane is a binary image, and additional gray levels are added as more bit planes are received. A lossless reconstruction is possible if all bit planes are used.

Since each bit plane is a binary image, binary compression techniques can be used to reduce the bit rate. (Refer to Chapter 6: Bit Plane Encoding for more details.) The amount of compression is largest for the most significant bit plane and decreases as one moves through the bit plane sequence. This property allows for large effective compression if the transmission is terminated after receiving the first few bit planes.

14.4.2   Tree-structured VQ

Progressive transmission can be achieved with a tree-structured VQ codebook by transmitting the index of the best-match intermediate codevector at each level of the tree [72]. As one progresses further into the tree, the reconstruction quality improves as the codevector choices become more refined. (Refer to Chapter 12 for a discussion of tree-structured codebooks and for examples of encoded images.) Tree-structured VQ provides lossy compression at the final level unless a residual error image is transmitted. Given the index of the codevector selected at a particular level, the specification of a codevector index at the next level requires an additional $\log_2 m$ bits, where m is the number of branches. Since these additional bits are distributed as overhead over the entire vector, the progressive transmission process is relatively efficient.

14.4.3   Transform-based hierarchical coding

In the section on transform coding, we discussed the ability of transforms to compact the image energy into a small number of coefficients. This property leads naturally to a hierarchical arrangement of the transform coefficients and allows for a recognizable reconstruction with a relatively small amount of data. Typically, the DCT is selected as the transform, although others, such as the Hadamard transform, may be used. Due to coefficient quantization, all of these techniques are lossy unless a residual error image is transmitted. The main distinction between various schemes is the method used to hierarchically order the coefficient information.

The most straightforward approach is to transmit the coefficients in order of approximately decreasing variance or in order of decreasing contribution to reconstructed image quality. This is generally accomplished by scanning a transformed block using a zigzag pattern (as in the JPEG DCT algorithm), but other scanning patterns have also been examined [73,74]. The partial information transmitted for each stage may be a single coefficient or a block of coefficients, and images are reconstructed by progressively including more of the coefficients in the inverse transform (with the unknown coefficients set to zero). This points to an obvious disadvantage of all transform-based techniques, namely, the need to perform an inverse transform at each step in the progression.

Rather than transmit only a few coefficients at each stage in the progression, another approach is to consider all of the coefficients within a given block and to allocate a limited number of bits to each one. As the progression proceeds, additional bits are added to each coefficient to improve the accuracy. One technique dynamically allocates a fixed number of bits at each stage and incorporates multistage quantization to iteratively refine any errors remaining from the previous stage [75]. Another technique uses embedded quantizers and predefined incremental bit maps to control the reconstruction quality at each stage [76].

14.5   Variable-Resolution Hierarchies

14.5.1   Subsampling pyramid

A spatial domain hierarchy can be generated by repeatedly subsampling the original image data. For example, the original $N \times N$ image could be subsampled by a factor of two in both dimensions, and then the resulting $N/2 \times N/2$ image could again be subsampled, and so on, until an image consisting of a single pixel is reached. The reconstruction process at any level simply uses the subsampled points from all previous levels plus the new points from the current level. The total number of stored pixel values is equivalent to that of the original image, and the original image can be recovered exactly. While this approach is efficient from this point of view, it suffers from several serious disadvantages. First, subsampling introduces aliasing, which becomes more pronounced at the higher levels of the pyramid. Second, the subsampled points may not be good representatives of the areas from which they are taken. Finally, it becomes difficult to apply compression techniques to the various levels because of the reduction in spatial correlation from the subsampling. However, these drawbacks may not be too severe in a system that requires only one or two hierarchical levels, and the subsampling approach may be worth considering for such a situation.

14.5.2   Mean pyramids

Forming a hierarchy by averaging over blocks of pixels (typically, 2×2 blocks) eliminates many of the problems associated with the subsampling approach. The use of averaging reduces the aliasing at higher levels of the pyramid (since the averaging acts as a prefilter), and the mean values are generally better representatives of the block regions. Although techniques based on a mean pyramid allow for a lossless reconstruction of the original image, they may result in data expansion depending on how the mean values are represented.

As an example, suppose we start with a k bits/pixel image and repeatedly average over 2×2 blocks to generate a full pyramid as shown in Fig. 14.1; i.e., we average until only a single value remains. If k bits are used to represent the means at each level, the total number of bits required to store the pyramid would be 33% more than that required for the original image [77]. Of course, the number of bits could be reduced by applying a variable-length code to the mean values, but the savings will generally be small. This is because the averaging process does not greatly affect the probability distribution of the pixel values (which is generally not highly skewed), and thus the entropy of this pyramid is approximately the same as the entropy of the original image. This type of pyramid has been termed the *truncated mean pyramid* [78].

The data expansion problem associated with averaging can be reduced by using a slightly more complex approach that increases the bit precision as one moves up the pyramid [77]. In this technique, the pyramid is generated by repeatedly forming sums, rather than averages, over 2×2 blocks. If k bits/pixel are used for the original image, then $k + 2$ bits are required to exactly represent each sum at the next level, $k + 4$ bits are required for each sum at the level above that, and so on. (The values used for display can be easily computed from the sums.) A reduction in storage is achieved by noting that given a sum from one level and three of its four components from the lower level, it is possible to recover the fourth component. Thus, we can discard one-quarter of the values at each level. This approach has been termed the *reduced-sum pyramid* [78]. The resulting number of values that must be stored is equal to the number of pixels in the original, but because of the increased bit precision needed for the sums, the total of bits required is approximately 8.3% more than the original for an 8-bit image [77]. As in the previous approach, variable-length coding would generally result in only a small savings.

Another approach that is more efficient than the reduced-sum pyramid in terms of coding performance is the *reduced-difference pyramid* [78]. In this technique, the truncated mean pyramid is formed as described previously;

i.e., repeatedly average over 2×2 blocks and use only k bits to represent each mean value at any level. At each level, differences are then formed between neighboring values within the 2×2 blocks. That is, if the four values within a block are x_1, x_2, x_3, and x_4, we form the differences

$$
\begin{aligned}
d_1 &= x_1 - x_2, \\
d_2 &= x_2 - x_3, \\
d_3 &= x_3 - x_4, \\
d_4 &= x_4 - x_1,
\end{aligned}
\tag{14.1}
$$

using $k + 1$ bits to represent each one. It is only necessary to retain three of the four difference values, since the other can be recovered given the three values and the corresponding mean from the next higher level. (Refer to [78] for the algorithm used to recover the data.) The resulting number of values that must be stored is equal to the number of pixels in the original image, but because $k + 1$ bits are required for each difference, the total number of bits is increased. (For an 8-bit image, the increase is 12.5%.) However, the difference values generated by this method have a substantially lower entropy than the original image (and also the truncated mean pyramid or the reduced-sum pyramid), and variable-length codes can be used to provide efficient storage of the pyramid [78]. As examples, the LENA and BOOTS images were encoded using the reduced-difference pyramid, and the entropies of the resulting difference values were computed. These results are shown in Table 14.1, along with the entropies of the original images. A range of entropies are given for the reduced-difference pyramid since different results are obtained, depending on which difference value triplet is encoded; i.e., variations in the vertical and horizontal pixel correlations affect the distributions of the difference values. It can be seen that the reduced-difference pyramid provides reasonable compression (although not quite as good as lossless DPCM) while permitting progressive reconstruction.

An approach that is similar to the reduced-difference pyramid is the *S-transform* [79-81]. As before, the mean values over 2×2 blocks are used to form the image at the next level of the pyramid. The following difference values are also computed for each 2×2 block:

$$
\begin{aligned}
d_1 &= \frac{1}{2}(x_1 + x_2 - x_3 - x_4), \\
d_2 &= \frac{1}{2}(x_1 - x_2 - x_3 + x_4), \\
d_3 &= x_1 - x_2 + x_3 - x_4.
\end{aligned}
\tag{14.2}
$$

These three difference values represent the additional information needed to resolve the mean value of a block into its original four pixel values x_1, x_2, x_3, and x_4. It can be shown that by retaining only k bits for the mean, $k + 1$ bits for d_1 and d_2, and $k + 2$ bits for d_3, a lossless reconstruction of the x_i values can be obtained. As in the reduced-difference pyramid, the number of values that must be stored is equal to the number of original pixel values while the number of stored bits is increased. (For an 8-bit image, the increase is approximately 16.7%.) However, the difference values formed using the S-transform can be encoded even more efficiently than those generated in the reduced-difference pyramid. The result is a slight gain in compression efficiency at the expense of an increased number of computations. Entropies given in Table 14.1 for the LENA and BOOTS images encoded using the S-transform illustrate this slight gain.

14.5.3   Knowlton's technique

A rather ingenious method of forming a spatial domain hierarchy was described by Knowlton [82]. This approach produces a pyramid similar to the mean pyramid by using a reversible transformation to map the original image values to a new set of values. The transformation takes adjacent pairs of k-bit pixel values and maps each k-bit pair into a k-bit "composite value" and a k-bit "differentiator." This 1-to-1 mapping can be done with a look-up table or with a relatively simple algorithm [83]. The pyramid levels are generated by repeating this mapping process on pairs of composite values, alternating between horizontal and vertical pairs from level to level. Note that since the transformation is reversible, the original image can be recovered exactly.

The composite value is roughly equivalent to the mean of the two pixels, while the differentiator is roughly equivalent to their difference, biased by the middle gray-scale value, e.g., 128 for an 8-bit image. During reconstruction, the differentiators allow a composite value at one level to be decomposed into two composite values for the next higher resolution level of the pyramid, and the composite values are then displayed. A disadvantage of Knowlton's technique is that the composite values generated by the mapping process are generally not the true means of the pixel pairs. Therefore, at the lower resolution levels of the pyramid, the composite values may not adequately represent the corresponding areas in the original image.

It is necessary to store the differentiators for each level as well as the composite value at the top of the pyramid. The number of differentiators that must be stored is equal to the number of pixels in the original image, and since k bits are used for each value, the total number of bits required for the pyramid is the same as for the original image. However, the distribution of the differentiators is nonuniform, and variable-length codes can be used to reduce the number of bits required for the pyramid [82]. This is illustrated in Table 14.1 for the LENA and BOOTS images. Two entropy values are reported since the formation of composite values can be initially started with either horizontally or vertically adjacent pixels. This is analogous to the variations in entropy achieved with the various difference value triplets generated by the reduced-difference pyramid. Knowlton's technique falls between the S-transform pyramid and the reduced-difference pyramid in terms of compression efficiency.

Technique	Entropy (bits/pixel)	
	LENA	**BOOTS**
Original image	7.45	7.49
Reduced-difference	$4.90 \rightarrow 5.05$	$5.66 \rightarrow 5.72$
S-transform	4.81	5.54
Knowlton	4.85, 4.99	5.61, 5.66

Table 14.1: Entropies for mean pyramid coding techniques.

14.5.4 Prediction/residual pyramid

In the prediction/residual approach to coding, we use a limited amount of data to form a prediction image and then subtract the prediction from the original image to form a residual image. We have already seen how this general approach can be used to advantage in techniques such as lossy plus lossless residual encoding and prediction/residual VQ. To further improve the efficiency and to provide a hierarchical structure, the prediction/residual process can be iterated at several different scales to create a pyramid of residuals, often called the *Laplacian pyramid* [84]. In the following, we first describe the Laplacian pyramid and then extend it to a more general prediction/residual pyramid.

To create the Laplacian pyramid, the original image is successively lowpass filtered and subsampled to produce a pyramid consisting of reduced resolution versions of the original. This pyramid has been termed the *Gaussian pyramid* since the lowpass filters examined in [84] were approximately Gaussian in shape. Each lowpass filtered image is then expanded (by upsampling and filtering) to the dimensions of the next level to provide a prediction image for that level. By subtracting these prediction images from their corresponding images in the Gaussian pyramid, a pyramid of residual images is created. This pyramid is termed the Laplacian pyramid because it is similar to the output produced by filtering the original image with a Laplacian (or equivalently, a difference-of-Gaussians) weighting function. Figure 14.2 illustrates the generation of the Gaussian and Laplacian pyramids.[1]

The information that is stored consists of the residual images as well as the lowest resolution image in the Gaussian pyramid (the base image). The total number of values that must be stored is 33% more than the number of original pixels, but the residual images have smaller variances and are less correlated than the original image, and can thus be encoded efficiently. In [84], encoding was performed by quantizing the base image and the residuals

---

[1]The pyramids were generated using a 5×5 lowpass filter with $a = 0.3$ as described in [84]. This filter is somewhat broader and flatter than a Gaussian.

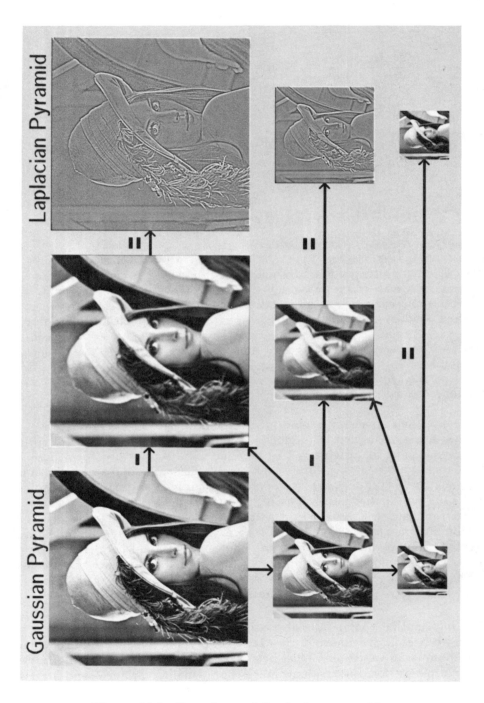

Figure 14.2: Gaussian and Laplacian pyramids.

and applying variable-length codes. The quantization levels were determined via simulations so that visual degradations in the reconstructed images were minimized.

Progressive reconstruction is achieved by starting with the base image, expanding to the dimensions of the next level, and adding in the corresponding residual to generate the next level in the Gaussian pyramid. This image is then expanded, added to its residual to create the next level, and so on. Each of the levels in the reconstructed Gaussian pyramid is available for display or output to an appropriate device. Since the Laplacian pyramid can be viewed as a set of bandpass-filtered versions of the original image [84], reconstruction of the Gaussian pyramid is equivalent to starting with a low-frequency representation (the base image) and then successively adding in additional higher frequency components (the residuals).

In the method just described, there is a fundamental asymmetry between the decomposition process and the reconstruction process. During decomposition, the residuals are generated using the full Gaussian pyramid created from the original, but during reconstruction, the only information available are the base image and the quantized residuals. Reconstruction is a recursive expansion process, starting with the base image, and quantization errors introduced at one level are propagated to all higher levels. Since the residuals were originally created assuming perfect reconstruction (i.e., they were created from the full Gaussian pyramid), there is no way to correct for these errors with this approach.

To overcome this problem, the asymmetry between the decomposition and the reconstruction processes can be eliminated, resulting in a more general prediction/residual approach. The basic idea in the decomposition process is to start with the base image, expand it to the next level to create a prediction image, and subtract it from the corresponding lowpass image to create a residual. This residual is quantized, added back to the expanded base image (the prediction image), and the result is then expanded to form the prediction image for the next level. The residual at this next level can also be quantized, added back to the corresponding prediction image, the resulting image expanded, and so on. In this way, any errors introduced at one level are taken into account at the next level. If the final residual is losslessly encoded, then the original image can be completely recovered.

It is worthwhile to note that the Gaussian pyramid can be generated using almost any lowpass filter (not necessarily Gaussian in shape) or even simple averaging. Since the images in the Gaussian pyramid are the ones that will be displayed, it is really up to the system designer to determine the level of quality needed at each level. Also, any interpolation method, including simple pixel replication, can be used to expand the image at one level up to the next level. Obviously, some methods will result in better prediction images, which lead to more efficient compression.

14.5.5   Hierarchical interpolation

A variation on the prediction/residual approach is to form the variable-resolution pyramid by strict subsampling, i.e., without any prefiltering, as described in Section 14.5.1. Residuals are then generated using the standard approach of interpolation and subtraction. This method has been termed HINT (Hierarchical INTerpolation) [85,86]. Forming the pyramid in this way has the advantage that when an image at one level is interpolated to the next higher resolution level, only the interpolated pixels need a residual in order to be reconstructed exactly since the subsampled pixels are already correct and hence need no residual. As a result, the total number of values that must be stored is equal to the number of original pixels, as compared to the 33% expansion for the Laplacian pyramid. Unfortunately, the use of subsampling with no prefiltering may yield images at the lower resolution levels that are unacceptable for display. This is because (1) aliasing artifacts are introduced by the subsampling process, and (2) the subsampled points may not be good representatives of the regions from which they have been taken. However, if a subsampling pyramid is necessary for a particular application, the HINT method does offer improved performance over the method described in Section 14.5.1 since the residuals can be stored more efficiently than the intermediate subsampled pixel values.

14.5.6   Subband pyramid

Subband coding using quadrature mirror filters (QMFs) provides a natural hierarchical structure that is quite similar to the Laplacian pyramid. (Refer to Chapter 13 for a discussion of the subband decomposition process.) Unlike the Laplacian pyramid, the number of values stored in the subband pyramid is the same as the number of pixels in the original image. The lowest frequency subband is a lowpass filtered and subsampled version of the original and is analogous to the base image in the Laplacian pyramid. The other subbands contain bands of higher frequency components, and they can loosely be interpreted as a more refined representation of the Laplacian residual image information. Reconstruction proceeds by using the lowest frequency subband as the initial approximation and then successively incorporating the higher frequency subbands by appropriate upsampling and filtering with QMFs. Due to quantization effects, subband coding typically results in a lossy reconstruction unless a final residual error image is included.

Chapter 15

Choosing a Lossy Compression Technique

The question "What is the *best* lossy compression algorithm?" is often asked, but unfortunately there is no absolute answer. The choice of a particular algorithm for a given application depends on many factors. For example, when compression is used in an image transmission application, the encoding and decoding operation often needs to be performed in real time, and the issues of implementation complexity, susceptibility to channel errors, and buffering requirements to match the coder output rate to the transmission rate of the channel become important. In contrast, in applications where compression is used to reduce storage requirements, the encoding operation often does not need to be performed in real time. The encoder can be quite complex since it will be used only once for a given image, while a simple decoder is desirable since it will be used repeatedly. Also, the error rates encountered in storage and retrieval applications are typically many orders of magnitude lower than the error rates for a communications channel. This may allow for a more sophisticated algorithm with greater emphasis placed on final image quality.

The following is a list of factors that can influence the choice of a compression algorithm. In general, the weighting of each factor in making a decision is highly dependent on the application. This list is by no means exhaustive, and is intended to serve only as a general guide.

- **Sensitivity to input image types**: Since we are focusing on compression algorithms for continuous-tone imagery, we will not discuss the robustness of these techniques for text or computer-generated imagery. Within the general class of continuous-tone imagery, input image characteristics such as dynamic range, image noise, frequency content, pixel-to-pixel correlation, and image resolution may all affect the performance and thus the choice of an algorithm. Also, some compression schemes may require parameter tuning to obtain good performance with a given class of images, and performance can significantly degrade if other types of input images are allowed. A particular example is any algorithm that relies on nonadaptive entropy coding, e.g., static Huffman coding, to provide a significant portion of the compression. If the statistics of the symbols to be encoded are roughly the same for most images, then a fixed (global) codebook may be used without incurring a significant penalty in the bit rate. On the other hand, if such statistics are not robust for different images, then either a local codebook must be generated (requiring two passes through the data) or one must accept the sometimes appreciable increase in bit rate due to the mismatch between the source and the codebook.

- **Operational bit rate**: In some applications, the priority is to achieve a very high degree of compression even at the cost of low image quality. In contrast, other applications may require a high degree of image quality that can only be achieved at modest compression ratios. Such requirements can severely limit the choice of the compression algorithm. In general, for the majority of compression schemes, there is a certain range of output bit rates for which the algorithm is most efficient, i.e., the range where it operates closest to the $R(D)$ curve (see Fig. 5.1). To achieve optimum results, it is desirable to keep the bit rate within that specified range. Beyond this basic principle, however, there are several other aspects that must be considered.

  First, by their very nature, some algorithms cannot be operated below a certain bit rate while other algorithms are quite costly to operate at high bit rates. For example, nonadaptive BTC can only operate at 2 bits/pixel unless additional source coding is used. Similarly, DPCM schemes do not inherently operate at fractional bit rates or at rates below one bit/pixel unless combined with entropy coding and/or implemented in a hybrid setting. Conversely, to achieve a bit rate ≥ 1 bit/pixel with the 16-band SBC technique using straight VQ, a codebook of size $\geq 2^{16}$ is required, which may become impractical.

  Second, some applications require a single compression algorithm to operate at varying bit rates or with different degrees of image quality. In such cases, it is desirable to have the ability to optimally and easily trade off the bit rate for the reconstructed image quality by adjusting a small set of compression parameters (which usually control the degree of quantization). An algorithm such as the JPEG DCT can inherently operate in this manner by varying the quantization normalization array, while others, such as DPCM or nonadaptive BTC, can operate at only a few specific bit rates (or even just one bit rate) and require a redesign of the system to achieve other bit rates.

- **Constant bit rate vs constant quality**: Algorithms that operate with a constant bit rate (such as VQ or DPCM with no entropy coding) are more suitable for transmission applications where a fixed rate channel with no buffering is used or for storage applications where the storage space is prespecified. Unfortunately, due to the wide variation in the information content of different images, such schemes do not result in constant reconstruction quality. The specified bit rate may be unnecessarily high for some images while resulting in unsatisfactory image quality for others. In contrast, some schemes maintain a constant visual quality or distortion measure, e.g., SNR, at the expense of a variable bit rate. This variable bit rate is often the result of including entropy coding in the scheme. The range over which the bit rate may vary is an important hardware consideration since adequate buffering must generally be provided. However, the availability of packet-switched networks has made variable-rate schemes somewhat more appealing in recent times for image transmission systems.

- **Implementation issues**: This refers to the nature and complexity of the algorithm relative to the particular hardware or software environment in which it is implemented. Three aspects of an algorithm need to be considered: (1) computational complexity, i.e., the per pixel number of additions, multiplications, shifts, comparisons, or other operations required, (2) memory requirements, and (3) amenability to parallel processing or other efficient processing structures. Typical implementation environments with current technology include PC-based, DSP (digital signal processor) chip-based, and ASIC (application specific integrated circuit)-based systems. The characteristics of each type of environment determines the suitability of an algorithm and the speed at which it can operate in that environment. It should be noted that the computational complexity results that have been presented for the different compression techniques are for the specific implementations described. Other implementations with different system parameters may significantly alter the number of required computations.

- **Encoder/decoder asymmetry**: Some approaches to compression inherently result in a complex encoder but a simple decoder (e.g., VQ), while others require an encoder and a decoder of comparable complexity (e.g., JPEG DCT). While encoders and decoders of equal complexity may be acceptable in many transmission applications, a simple decoder is more desirable in applications where it is repeatedly used such as image storage and retrieval systems. As described previously, the inclusion of adaptivity can also significantly alter this balance as well as increase the overall complexity of the system.

- **Channel error tolerance**: Unfortunately, one of the prices paid for data compression is the increased susceptibility of encoded data to channel errors, and the degree of susceptibility varies widely among the different schemes. In case of block processing algorithms (e.g., BTC or DCT), the effect of a bit error is often confined to only a small block of the image, while in other schemes it appears as a streak across the image (e.g., DPCM). If variable-length coding is used, which is often the case in more sophisticated schemes, the effect of channel errors can be catastrophic and can result in the loss of the whole image.

Of course, error control coding can be added to any system, but the price to be paid is an increase in the overall complexity and bit rate.

- **Artifacts**: Different algorithms create different artifacts depending on their mode of operation. Even a given algorithm may exhibit different artifacts depending on the bit rate at which it is operated. Some artifacts such as blocking or edge jaggedness may be visually more objectionable than random noise or overall edge smoothing. Also, the visibility of artifacts is highly dependent on the particular image and the conditions under which it is viewed.

- **Effect of multiple coding**: Some applications may require that an image undergo the compression-decompression cycle many times. For example an image may be compressed and transmitted to a destination where it is decompressed and viewed. An operator may alter a small portion of the image and then compress the whole image and send it to another destination where this process is further repeated. In such applications, it is essential that the repeated compression and decompression of the unaltered portions does not result in any additional degradation beyond the first stage of compression. Some compression schemes do not create further loss of image quality when successively used on the same image, while others cause additional degradations. Fortunately, in most cases, subsequent losses are significantly less than the loss caused by the first stage.

- **Progressive transmission capability**: Progressive image transmission allows for an approximate image to be sent at a low bit rate for quick recognition, and then remaining details are transmitted incrementally if desired by the user. Of course, any scheme can artificially be made progressive by using it to encode a low-resolution version of the original image as a first approximation and then encoding the difference between this stage and either the original image or another intermediate stage to create as many levels of progression as desired. As described in Chapter 14: Hierarchical Coding, some schemes are inherently amenable to progressive transmission due to the embedded structure of the encoder and can operate in that mode without requiring any additional complexity. Other techniques can also operate in a progressive mode but at the expense of additional system complexity.

- **System compatibility**: If the system requires compatibility with other maufacturers' products, then the choice of a compression scheme may be dictated by the existence of standards that have been proposed and/or adopted, e.g., CCITT facsimile standards or JPEG-proposed continuous-tone color image compression algorithm [33].

15.1 Bit Rate/Quality Performance Summary

In this section, we summarize the bit rate/quality performance of the specific implementations we have described in the preceding chapters on lossy compression techniques. This summary is done in the form of plots of PSNR vs bit rate for the two test images, LENA and BOOTS, shown in Figs. 15.1 and 15.2, respectively. Our intent is not to choose the "best" algorithm based on these plots, for as we have seen, many factors besides bit rate/quality are involved in making such a choice. The intent is merely to provide a convenient summary and comparison of *typical* bit rates and error measures for the various approaches to lossy compression.

As noted in previous chapters, the use of PSNR (or equivalently, RMSE) as a measure of image quality is certainly not ideal since it generally does not correlate well with perceived image quality. Nevertheless, it is commonly used in the evaluation of compression techniques, and it does provide some measure of relative performance. The reconstructed images of LENA we have included in the text should allow the reader to get a feel for the subjective quality achieved by the different techniques, but it should be noted that limitations of the printing process can hide certain details that might be obvious using a different display medium.

Ideally, it would be desirable to run all algorithms at a few specific bit rates and compare the resulting subjective and objective image quality. However, this is not possible because of the inherent nature of some of the algorithms. (Refer to discussion on operational bit rates under the factors in choosing an algorithm.) The adopted approach was to run the algorithms within their typical range of operation, and if possible, at the specific bit rates of 0.50, 1.00, and 2.00 bits/pixel. In cases where this was not possible, the effort has been to achieve bit rates reasonably close to these values.

Once again, it is worth emphasizing that the results presented in this chapter are for *specific implementations* of general techniques and for *specific images* within a general class of images. Better performance can generally be obtained by including additional complexity, and the performance of any given algorithm can vary greatly with the type of image being encoded.

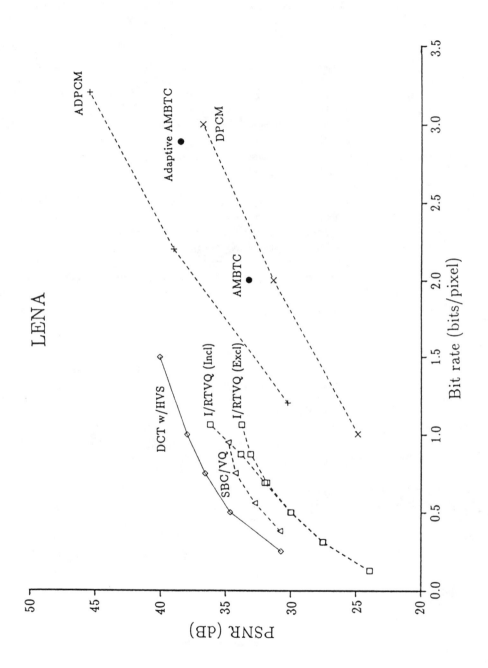

Figure 15.1: PSNR vs bit rate for LENA.

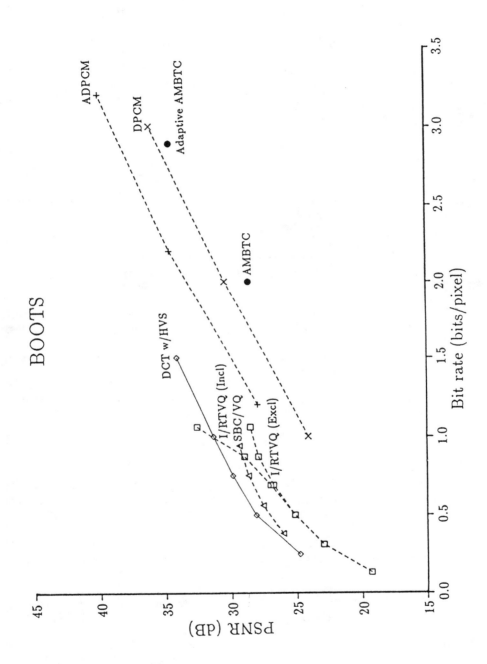

Figure 15.2: PSNR vs bit rate for BOOTS.

References

[1] A. Habibi, "Comparison of nth-order DPCM encoder with linear transformations and block quantization techniques," IEEE Trans. Commun. Tech., COM-19(6), 948-956 (1971).

[2] H. G. Musmann, "Predictive image coding," in *Image Transmission Techniques*, W. K. Pratt, ed., *Advances in Electronics and Electron Physics*, Supplement 12, 73-112, Academic Press, Orlando, FL (1979).

[3] S. E. Elnahas, "Data compression with applications to digital radiology," D.Sc. dissertation, Washington Univ., St. Louis, MO (1984).

[4] A. Rosenfeld and A. C. Kak, *Digital Picture Processing*, Vol. 1, Academic Press, Orlando, FL (1982).

[5] A. K. Jain, *Fundamentals of Digital Image Processing*, 491-494, Prentice-Hall, Englewood Cliffs, NJ (1989).

[6] A. N. Netravali, "On quantizers for DPCM coding of picture signals," IEEE Trans. Info. Theory, IT-23(3), 360-370 (1977).

[7] J. O. Limb and C. B. Rubinstein, "On the design of quantizers for DPCM coders: a functional relationship between visibility, probability, and masking," IEEE Trans. Commun., COM-26(5), 573-578 (1978).

[8] D. K. Sharma and A. N. Netravali, "Design of quantizers for DPCM coding of picture signals," IEEE Trans. Commun., COM-25(11), 1267-1274 (1978).

[9] A. N. Netravali and B. Prasada, "Adaptive quantization of picture signals using spatial masking," Proc. IEEE, 65(4), 536-548 (1977).

[10] S. P. Lloyd, "Least squares quantization in PCM," Bell Lab. Memo, July 1957; also in IEEE Trans. Info. Theory, IT-28, 129-137 (1982).

[11] J. Max, "Quantizing for minimum distortion," IRE Trans. Info. Theory, IT-6(1), 7-12 (1960).

[12] T. Berger, "Optimum quantizers and permutation codes," IEEE Trans. Info. Theory, IT-18(6), 754-755 (1972).

[13] R. C. Wood, "On optimum quantization," IEEE Trans. Info. Theory, IT-15(2), 248-252 (1969).

[14] J. B. O'Neal, "Entropy coding in speech and television differential PCM systems," IEEE Trans. Info. Theory, IT-17, 758-761 (1971).

[15] P. Kabal, "Quantizers for the Gamma distribution and other symmetrical distributions," IEEE Trans. Acous., Speech, Signal Proc., ASSP-32(4), 836-841 (1984).

[16] H. Yamaguchi, "Optimum quantization of Laplace density signal and its characteristics," Electronics and Communications in Japan, 67-B, 5, 67-73 (1984).

[17] A. N. Netravali and J. O. Limb, "Picture coding: A review," Proc. IEEE, 68(3), 366-406 (1980).

[18] M. Rabbani, L. A. Ray, and J. R. Sullivan, "Adaptive predictive coding with applications to radiographs," Medical Instrumentation, 20, 182-191 (1986).

[19] W. Zschunke, "DPCM picture coding with adaptive prediction," IEEE Trans. Commun., COM-25(11), 1295-1302 (1977).

[20] K. Yamada, K. Kinukaba, and H. Sasaki, Int. Conf. Commun. Rec., 1, 76-80 (1977).

[21] N. S. Jayant, "Adaptive quantization with a one-word memory," Bell Syst. Tech. J., 52, 1119-1144 (1973).

[22] D. Anastassiou, W. B. Pennebaker, and J. L. Mitchell, "Gray-scale image coding for freeze-frame videoconferencing," IEEE Trans. Commun., COM-34(4), 382-394 (1986).

[23] P. J. Ready and D. J. Spencer, "Block adaptive DPCM transmission of images," in *NTC Conference Record*, 2, 22-10 - 22-17 (1975).

[24] A. Habibi and B. H. Batson, "Potential digitization/compression techniques for shuttle video," IEEE Trans. Commun., COM-26(11), 1671-1682 (1978).

[25] J. R. Sullivan, "A new ADPCM image compression algorithm and the effect of fixed-pattern sensor noise," in *Proc. SPIE Digital Image Processing Applications*, 1075, 129-138 (1989).

[26] W. K. Pratt, *Digital Image Processing*, Wiley-Interscience, New York (1978).

[27] E. O. Brigham, *The Fast Fourier Transform*, Prentice-Hall, Englewood Cliffs, NJ (1974).

[28] W. H. Chen and W. K. Pratt, "Scene adaptive coder," IEEE Trans. Commun., COM-32(3), 224-232 (1984).

[29] R. J. Clarke, *Transform Coding of Images*, Academic Press, London (1985).

[30] A. Habibi and P. A. Wintz, "Image coding by linear transformation and block quantization," IEEE Trans. Commun. Tech., COM-19(1), 50-63 (1971).

[31] W. H. Chen and C. H. Smith, "Adaptive coding of monochrome and color images," IEEE Trans. Commun., COM-25(11), 1285-1292 (1977).

[32] A. Habibi, "Survey of adaptive image coding techniques," IEEE Trans. Commun., COM-25(11), 1275-1284 (1977).

[33] W. Pennebaker, "JPEG Technical Specification, Revision 8," Working Document No. JTC1/SC2/WG10/JPEG-8-R8 (Aug. 1990).

[34] C. A. Gonzales and J. L. Mitchell, "A note on DCT algorithms with low multiplicative complexity," JPEG-150 (1988).

[35] M. Vetterli, "Fast 2-D discrete cosine transform," in *Proc. ICASSP*, 1538-1541 (1985).

[36] E. Feig, "A fast scaled-DCT algorithm," in *Proc. SPIE Image Processing Algorithms and Techniques*, 1244, 2-13 (1990).

[37] B. G. Lee, "A new algorithm to compute the discrete cosine transform," IEEE Trans. Acous., Speech, Signal Proc., ASSP-32(6), 1243-1245 (1984).

[38] M. Vetterli and H. Nussbaumer, "Simple FFT and DCT algorithms with reduced number of operations," Signal Processing, 6, 267-278 (1984).

[39] Y. Arai, T. Agui, and M. Nakajima, "A fast DCT-SQ scheme for images," Trans. IEICE, E-71, 1095-1097 (1988).

[40] O. R. Mitchell, E. J. Delp, and S. G. Carlton, "Block truncation coding: a new approach to image compression," in *Proc. ICC*, 12B.1.1-12B.1.4 (1978).

[41] E. J. Delp and O. R. Mitchell, "Some aspects of moment preserving quantizers," in *Proc. ICC*, 7.2.1-7.2.5 (1979).

[42] E. J. Delp and O. R. Mitchell, "Image compression using block truncation coding," IEEE Trans. Commun., COM-27(9), 1135-1342 (1979).

[43] D. R. Halverson, "On the implementation of a block truncation coding algorithm," IEEE Trans. Commun., COM-30(11), 2482-2484 (1982).

[44] D. R. Halverson, N. C. Griswold, and G. L. Wise, "A generalized block truncation coding algorithm for image compression," IEEE Trans. Acous., Speech, Signal Proc., ASSP-32(3), 664-668 (1984).

[45] N. C. Griswold, D. R. Halverson, and G. L. Wise, "A note on adaptive block truncation coding for image processing," IEEE Trans. Acous., Speech, Signal Proc., ASSP-35(8), 1201-1203 (1987).

[46] O. R. Mitchell and E. J. Delp, "Multilevel graphics representation using block truncation coding," Proc. IEEE, 68(7), 868-873 (1980).

[47] D. J. Healy and O. R. Mitchell, "Digital video bandwidth compression using block truncation coding," IEEE Trans. Commun., COM-29(12), 1809-181 (1981).

[48] M. D. Lema and O. R. Mitchell, "Absolute moment block truncation coding and its application to color images," IEEE Trans. Commun., COM-32(10), 1148-1157 (1984).

[49] V. R. Udpikar and J. P. Raina, "BTC image coding using vector quantization," IEEE Trans. Commun., COM-35(3), 352-356 (1987).

[50] S. Murakami, E. Mitsuya, K. Mori, T. Kishimoto, and T. Kamae, "One bit/pel coding of still pictures," in *Proc. ICC*, 23.1.1-23.1.5 (1979).

[51] Y. Linde, A. Buzo, and R. M. Gray, "An algorithm for vector quantizer design," IEEE Trans. Commum., COM-28(1), 84-95 (1980).

[52] R. M. Gray, "Vector quantization," IEEE ASSP Magazine, 1(2), 4-29 (1984).

[53] W. H. Equitz, "A new vector quantization clustering algorithm," IEEE Trans. Acous., Speech, Signal Proc., ASSP-37(10), 1568-1575 (1989).

[54] J. Makhoul, S. Roucos, and H. Gish, "Vector quantization in speech coding," Proc. IEEE, 73(11), 1551-1588 (1985).

[55] R. L. Baker, "Vector quantization of digital images," Ph.D. thesis, Department of Electrical Engineering, Stanford University, 170-175 (June 1984).

[56] P. A. Chou, T. Lookabaugh, and R. M. Gray, "Optimal pruning with applications to tree-structured source coding and modeling," IEEE Trans. Info. Theory, 35(2), 299-315 (1989).

[57] R. L. Baker and R. M. Gray, "Differential vector quantization of achromatic imagery," in *Proc. Int. Picture Coding Symposium*, 105-106 (1983).

[58] H.-M. Hang and B. Haskell, "Interpolative vector quantization of color images," IEEE Trans. Commun., COM-36(4), 465-470 (1988).

[59] B. Ramamurthi and A. Gersho, "Classified vector quantization of images," IEEE Trans. Commun., COM-34(11), 1105-1115 (1986).

[60] J. Foster, R. M. Gray, and M. O. Dunham, "Finite-state vector quantization for waveform coding," IEEE Trans. Info. Theory, IT-31(3), 348-359 (1985).

[61] P. P. Vaidyanathan, "Quadrature mirror filter banks, M-band extensions and perfect-reconstruction techniques," IEEE ASSP Magazine, 4(3), 4-20 (1987).

[62] J. D. Johnston, "A filter family designed for use in quadrature mirror filter banks," in *Proc. ICASSP*, 291-294 (1980).

[63] C. R. Galand and H. J. Nussbaumer, "New quadrature mirror filter structures," IEEE Trans Acous., Speech, Signal Proc., ASSP-32(3), 522-530 (1984).

[64] E. H. Adelson, E. Simoncelli, and R. Hingorani, "Orthogonal pyramid transforms for image coding," in *Proc. SPIE Visual Communications and Image Processing II*, 845, 50-58 (1987).

[65] M. J. T. Smith and T. P. Barnwell, "Exact reconstruction techniques for tree-structured subband coders," IEEE Trans. Acous., Speech, Signal Proc., ASSP-34(3), 434-441 (1986).

[66] D. Le Gall and A. Tabatabai, "Sub-band coding of digital images using symmetric kernel filters and arithmetic coding techniques," in *Proc. ICASSP*, 761-764 (1988).

[67] J. W. Woods and S. D. O'Neil, "Subband coding of images," IEEE Trans. Acous. Speech Signal Processing, ASSP-34(5), 1278-1288 (1986).

[68] J. C. Darragh, "Subband and transform coding of images," Ph.D. thesis, Department of Electrical Engineering, UCLA, 72-75 (1989).

[69] H. Gharavi and A. Tabatabai, "Sub-band coding of monochrome and color images," IEEE Trans. Circuits Systems, 35(2), 207-214 (1988).

[70] P. H. Westerink, D. E. Boekee, J. Biemond, and J. W. Woods, "Subband coding of images using vector quantization," IEEE Trans. Commun., COM-36(6), 713-719 (1988).

[71] D. M. Baylon and J. S. Lim, "Transform/subband analysis and synthesis of signals," MIT Research Laboratory of Electronics Technical Report (June 1990).

[72] M. I. Sezan, M. Rabbani, and P. W. Jones, "Progressive transmission of images using a prediction/residual encoding approach," Opt. Eng., 28(5), 556-564 (1989).

[73] K. N. Ngan, "Image display techniques using the cosine transform," IEEE Trans. Acous., Speech, Signal Proc., ASSP-32(1), 173-177 (1984).

[74] E. Dubois and J. L. Moncet, "Encoding and progressive transmission of still pictures in NTSC composite format using transform domain methods," IEEE Trans. Commun., COM-34(3), 310-319 (1986).

[75] L. Wang and M. Goldberg, "Progressive image transmission by transform coefficient residual error quantization," IEEE Trans. Commun., COM-36(1), 75-87 (1988).

[76] S. E. Elnahas, K. H. Tzou, J. R. Cox, R. L. Hill, and R. G. Gilbert, "Progressive coding and transmission of digital diagnostic pictures," IEEE Trans. Medical Imag., MI-5(2), 73-83 (1986).

[77] S. L. Tanimoto, "Image transmission with gross information first," Comput. Graphics and Image Proc., 9, 72-76 (1979).

[78] L. Wang and M. Goldberg, "Reduced-difference pyramid: a data structure for progressive image transmission," Opt. Eng., 28(7), 708-716 (1989).

[79] ACR/NEMA Standards Publication for Data Compression Standards, NEMA Publication PS-2, Washington, DC (1989).

[80] P. Lux, "Redundancy reduction in radiographic pictures," Opt. Acta, 24(4), 349-365 (1977).

[81] H. Blume and A. Fand, "Reversible and irreversible image data compression using the S-transform and Lempel-Ziv coding," in *Proc. SPIE Medical Imaging III: Image Capture and Display*, 1091, 2-18 (1989).

[82] K. Knowlton, "Progressive transmission of grey-scale and binary pictures by simple, efficient, and lossless encoding schemes," Proc. IEEE, 68(7), 885-896 (1980).

[83] F. S. Hill, S. Walker, and F. Gao, "Interactive image query system using progressive transmission," Comput. Graphics, 17(3), 323-333 (1983).

[84] P. J. Burt and E. H. Adelson, "The Laplacian pyramid as a compact image code," IEEE Trans. Commun., COM-31(4), 532-540 (1983).

[85] T. Endoh and T. Yamazaki, "Progressive coding scheme for multi level images," in *Proc. Picture Coding Symposium*, 21-22 (1986).

[86] P. Roos, A. Viergever, M. C. A. van Dijke, and J. H. Peters, "Reversible intraframe compression of medical images," IEEE Trans. Medical Imag., 7(4), 328-336 (1988).

Appendix A

Compression of Color Images

All of the image compression techniques described in this book have assumed single-band, i.e., monochrome, images. In many imaging applications, it is necessary to deal with color or multispectral images. Typically, a color image is represented by three bands (or planes), corresponding to red, green, and blue tristimulus values, denoted $R(i,j)$, $G(i,j)$, and $B(i,j)$, respectively, at each pixel location (i,j). In some applications, such as remote sensing via satellites, an image may contain substantially more than three bands in order to provide information over a wide range of wavelengths.

Extending the compression techniques to color images can be done easily by encoding each band independently using the same technique. Unfortunately, this simple approach is generally not optimal in terms of providing the most efficient compression. This is because there is often substantial correlation between the various color planes, and this redundancy is not removed by the independent processing of the planes. The correlation is mainly due to the fact that typical scenes are characterized by smooth spectral reflectances and partly because the spectral shape of the tristimulus color sensitivity functions overlap.

To achieve efficient compression with color images, the problem can be approached in two different ways: one based on the statistical properties of the color planes, and another based on the HVS encoding and perception of color. In the following, we briefly explain each of the two different approaches.

A.1   Statistical Spectral Compression

Consider a multispectral image consisting of M bands, e.g., an RGB color image where $M = 3$, or a reconnaissance image with M different bands. Let us denote each composite pixel value by the M-dimensional vector $\mathbf{X}(i,j)$, where each component of the vector correponds to a certain spectral band; e.g., for a RGB color image, $\mathbf{X}(i,j) = [R(i,j), G(i,j), B(i,j)]$. Due to the correlations between the spectral bands, the M-dimensional scatter diagram constructed by plotting the vector components for all pixel locations exhibits clustering along certain axes (similar to the 2-D plot of Fig. 10.2).

To exploit these correlations, a rotation of the coordinate axes can be performed to transform the vector $\mathbf{X}$ into a vector $\mathbf{Y}$ whose components are uncorrelated (see Chapter 10: Transform Coding). The transformed spectral planes are then separately encoded as monochrome images. The transformation generally aims at packing a large fraction of the spectral energy into a small number of transformed spectral planes, so the majority of the transform planes would contain little energy and can be encoded at very low bit rates. The optimum transform in terms of maximum energy compaction is the KLT (refer to Section 10.3.1), which unfortunately is image-dependent. To avoid the computational complexity associated with the KLT, an image-independent transform with reasonable decorrelating capability can be chosen for the class of imagery being encoded.

Another approach that uses the spectral correlation is based on VQ encoding [1] (refer to Chapter 12: Vector Quantization). By treating each composite pixel value as a vector, a codebook can be developed by either using the particular image or a series of images representing that class of imagery as a training set (local or global codebooks). The image vectors can also be formed as a combination of spectral and spatial components; e.g., a 12-dimensional vector can be formed using a 2×2 ($\times$ 3 channel) block of an RGB color image.

A.2   HVS Color Encoding

In some applications, it is impractical or undesirable to include a spectral transformation in the system due to the additional complexity. If the final image is to be viewed by a human observer, however, additional compression can often be achieved without a transform by making use of properties of the HVS. This is accomplished by compressing the color planes independently but with a different set of compression parameters for each plane to take advantage of variations in the HVS contrast sensitivity functions for different wavelengths. In this way, errors are introduced where the HVS is the least sensitive. For example, the blue color plane can often be compressed 25% more than the green color plane without creating any visual artifacts.

If the system complexity does allow for a spectral transformation, the HVS can also be used to guide the selection of a transform. The selection of a transform requires accurate models both for HVS color encoding and for color perception [2] in order to take best advantage of the HVS in compressing color images. Unfortunately, due to the complexities of the visual system, much controversy exists among the researchers in both areas. Loosely speaking, psychophysical experiments suggest that the visual system encodes color by transforming the output of the three cone color mechanisms into an achromatic channel (such as luminance) and two chromatic channels (opponent channels). This transform appears to approximately decorrelate the initial three-component data as described in the previous section. In perceiving color given this encoded data, the HVS is much more sensitive to variations in the achromatic channel than in the chromatic channels. These properties suggest a compression scheme where the RGB channels are first transformed into an achromatic channel and two chromatic channels, and then the achromatic channel is encoded with high fidelity while larger errors are allowed in the chromatic channels.

In most color compression schemes, the transforms used to generate the luminance and chrominance channels are linear combinations of the sensor output values; e.g., for the luminance channel,

$$Y(i,j) = w_1 R(i,j) + w_2 G(i,j) + w_3 B(i,j), \qquad (A.1)$$

where the weighting factors, w_1, w_2, and w_3, generally depend on the output device, the viewing conditions, and the HVS color perception model. An example of such a transform is that used in the NTSC national color television standard [3]. The RGB values are transformed into YIQ (luminance, in-phase, and quadrature, respectively) components according to the following transformation:

$$\begin{bmatrix} Y(i,j) \\ I(i,j) \\ Q(i,j) \end{bmatrix} = \begin{bmatrix} 0.299 & 0.587 & 0.114 \\ 0.596 & -0.274 & -0.322 \\ 0.212 & -0.523 & 0.311 \end{bmatrix} \begin{bmatrix} R(i,j) \\ G(i,j) \\ B(i,j) \end{bmatrix}.$$

In this case, the weighting factors used to form the luminance are based on an NTSC predefined output device. For a typical NTSC bandlimited color picture, this spectral conversion also has the desirable property of packing most of the signal energy into the Y plane (as much as 93%), and significantly less energy into the I ($\sim$ 5%) and Q ($\sim$ 2%) planes. For the purposes of image compression, the I and Q chrominance planes are often spatially averaged and subsampled by a factor of 2:1 or 4:1 in both the horizontal and vertical directions to take advantage of the reduced bandwidth of the HVS for these components. They can then be encoded using any of the conventional compression schemes. At the receiver, the reconstructed I and Q planes are interpolated back to their original size. The transformation to convert YIQ back to RGB is

$$\begin{bmatrix} R(i,j) \\ G(i,j) \\ B(i,j) \end{bmatrix} = \begin{bmatrix} 1.000 & 0.956 & 0.621 \\ 1.000 & -0.272 & -0.647 \\ 1.000 & -1.106 & 1.703 \end{bmatrix} \begin{bmatrix} Y(i,j) \\ I(i,j) \\ Q(i,j) \end{bmatrix}.$$

A transform that is similar to the YIQ transform, but easier to implement in hardware, is the color difference transform, which generates Y, $R - Y$, and $B - Y$ components. The perfect transform has yet to be agreed upon, but in our opinion, the performance differences are insignificant with respect to image compression.

References

[1] N. M. Nasrabadi and R. A. King, "Image coding using vector quantization: a review," IEEE Trans. Commun., 36(8), 957-971 (1988).

[2] L. M. Hurvich, *Color Vision*, Sinauer Associates, Sunderland, MA (1981).

[3] R. W. G. Hunt, *The Reproduction of Colour*, Fountain Press, England, Fourth edition (1987).

About the Authors

Majid Rabbani received his M.S. and Ph.D. degrees in electrical engineering from the University of Wisconsin at Madison in 1980 and 1983, respectively. He joined the Eastman Kodak Research Laboratories, Rochester, NY, in 1983, where he currently is the head of the image restoration and coding group. He is also an adjunct faculty at the department of electrical engineering at Rochester Institute of Technology (RIT). Dr. Rabbani has taught many short courses in the area of digital image processing. He is the recipient of the 1988 Kodak C. E. K. Mees Award (Kodak's highest research honor) for excellence in research. His current research interests include digital signal processing and image processing where he has published over 30 technical articles and holds six patents.

Paul W. Jones received the B.S. and M.S. degrees in imaging and photographic science from the Rochester Institute of Technology, Rochester, NY, in 1982 and the M.S. degree in electrical engineering from Rensselaer Polytechnic Institute, Troy, NY, in 1984. From 1980 to 1982, he was a physicist with the Xerox Corporation, Webster, NY, working on image quality issues, digital image simulation, and imaging systems analysis. Since 1984, he has been with the Eastman Kodak Company, Rochester, NY, working on digital image coding, restoration, and simulation, and is currently a senior research scientist. He holds five patents in the field of digital image coding and has published several papers in this same area.